VISION AND POLICY IN NIGERIAN ECONOMICS: THE LEGACY OF PIUS OKIGBO

Edited by

Jane I. Guyer and LaRay Denzer

West African Studies Series
Centre for Social Science Research and Development (CSSR&D)
Ikorodu, Lagos, Nigeria.

Ibadan University Press
Publishing House
University of Ibadan
Ibadan, Nigeria

First Published 2005

ISBN: 978 – 121 – 401 – 5
ISBN-13: 978 - 978 - 121 - 401 - 1

Printed by Lightning Source

CONTENTS

PART IV: INTELLECTUALS, PUBLIC LEADERSHIP AND CIVIL SOCIETY

APPENDICES

PREFACE

Jane I. Guyer

BACKGROUND TO THE CONFERENCE

On June 8–9, 2001, the Program of African Studies (PAS) convened a meeting to discuss the work of Pius Okigbo, who in 1956 became Northwestern University's first African recipient of a doctoral degree. The sad news of his death in September 2000 served, for us who knew him primarily by reputation alone, to shine a new spotlight of attention on his thought and on the issues to which he devoted his long and illustrious career in economic policy. Our first goal – to memorialize him and honour the long list of African scholars who have followed him through our graduate programs over the years -- was quickly expanded to encompass an intense engagement with the present and the future. The subjects of his research turned out to be as current today, and the debates about them as impassioned, as they were when he launched his career in Nigeria in 1958 in the heat of the nationalist moment immediately before Independence (1960). In fact, the topics on which he wrote well before the outbreak of the Civil War in 1966 have been at the centre of a rising crescendo of attention: fiscal federalism, the principles of derivation, regional integration and the probit of public institutions. Moreover, the encompassing issue of the appropriate place of the state in economic development is as controversial now as it was when Okigbo worked with Wolfgang Stolper on the first development plan. As Stolper's contribution shows, their philosophies differed at the time. But, as Adibe's paper argues in particular detail, those differences have proved themselves still relevant as poles for animated discussion.

How were we made aware of this sense of current relevance of Okigbo's opus as a catalyst for today's debates? The answer is: By the sheer enthusiasm of the response we received to our proposition. We had planned to run a fairly local, Chicago-and-region, one-day, somewhat modest, discussion. And then many people from much further away – including Nigeria

– offered to come, to write papers, to share recollections, to offer insights and above all, to engage again with the issues he raised. His former student colleague, Professor Sterling Stuckey, wanted to attend from California. Dr. Sylvester Ugoh came from Nigeria. Pius Okigbo Jr. represented the family, flying in from London. Professor Bede Okigbo planned to be there but was prevented at the last minute by visa difficulties. Professor Wolfgang Stolper wrote a paper, in spite of his advancing age (he passed away less than year later). Ambassador Arthur Mbanefo honoured us with his presence from the United Nations and delivered the keynote address. Others came to participate from various corners of the United States, including Richard A. Joseph, professor of political science at Emory University, scholar of Nigerian politics, who will take over the directorship of PAS in 2003, now that I have stepped down. This, indeed, was the last conference of my directorship and I now like to think of it as being the one at which the collective energy of the moment ensured the passing on of the NU/PAS baton from Guyer to Joseph (via the able administration of acting director during 2001–03, David Schoenbrun).

Rather than introduce the papers presented at the conference, I would prefer to recapitulate my introductory remarks to the opening session. I leave graduate student Henry Dougan to offer the next generation's 'take' on the proceedings. My first pleasure was to extend the welcome of our president Henry Bienen, himself a scholar of Nigeria, to the participants. His absence at the opening on Friday was more than compensated by his presence and spirited participation, straight from the airport, in the afternoon session on Saturday.

OKIGBO AND NORTHWESTERN UNIVERSITY

Why did we want to hold this meeting at all, so far from the arenas of Professor Okigbo's life's work? It is because, on the sad occasion of his death, we at Northwestern University wanted to *reclaim* him. And we wanted to reclaim him in several different capacities: as a person, as a representative of all our African students (past and present), and as a source of ever-relevant ideas about the future of Nigeria and of Africa. Let me expand briefly on each of these overlapping reasons:

First, as a person: we remember with great pleasure Pius Okigbo's enthusiastic presence at the jubilee celebration for the Program of African Studies in 1998. He heard about it and decided to attend from Nigeria. We were delighted and deeply moved. I remember him sitting close to the front at the opening presentations for our exhibit on the research of founder Melville Herskovits (whom, of course, he knew), and I particularly remember the look of pure enjoyment on his face. His presence gave us courage and validation in the value of our efforts. In our obituary in *PAS News and Events* we reprinted a photo of him in the Block Museum gallery with Jean Herskovits (daughter of Melville), myself and professor of art history, Ikem Okoye, who is also from Eastern Nigeria. Professor Okigbo seems in mid-speech, doubtless making one of the apposite amusing comments to which so many of his memorial tributes in Nigeria drew attention. *We* certainly look amused! He came for one reason: he was an alumnus of Northwestern: MA and Ph.D. in Economics, graduating in 1956, in the exciting period between the constitutional reforms that created regional self-government in Nigeria and the achievement of full independence in 1960. He was a leading member of the pioneer generation of Nigerian professional public servants. The interweaving of political structures and economic dynamics that were so clear in that constitutional period became his life's work.

But secondly, for us at Northwestern, Professor Okigbo was more than a delightful colleague whose career coincided with great changes in his country. He also represents the achievements of *all* our African doctoral graduates, because he was the first. He was recruited through the new national and university efforts that followed World War II to attract and support African students. Among those with whom he overlapped here were his friend Kofi Tetteh, retired chief justice of Botswana, and Eduardo Mondlane, freedom-fighter and nation-builder of Mozambique. This was only the beginning. Northwestern University has graduated dozens of African scholars and professionals over the years. For the period between 1956 and 1988, we can enumerate at least thirty who became influential in national and international affairs, including one head of state in addition to Mondlane, numerous diplomats, directors of research institutes, senior public servants, professors, and important contributors to a variety of walks of life. In American academia, each discipline's ranking in its field depends in part on the achievements of its graduates, but mainly their achievements in *American* life, where these are easy to document and to measure. It is arguable, however, that our *foreign* graduates have broken all records of achievement, even though they hardly figure in the disciplinary tallies. So we take this opportunity, when we review the career and the ideas of Pius Okigbo, to see him as a trailblazer and a symbol for *all* of the African graduates of Northwestern University who have contributed so much to scholarship and public life in their own countries and beyond.

Thirdly, there is another symbolic value that Pius Okigbo represents for us here at Northwestern, and that is the value of our relationship to Nigeria. It is an accident of history that our first Ph.D. was Nigerian, but it marked the beginning of Northwestern's strong connections to his country. At least three of the six directors of the Program of African Studies, and two interim directors, have carried out research in Nigeria, including myself. In addition, at least four other current faculty have published works on Nigeria. At least three of our current faculty and staff, including President Bienen, have been faculty at Nigerian universities. During my tenure here, two Northwestern faculty have been Nigerian by origin. Over the years, many of our graduates have been Nigerians, two of whom, Hamidu Bobboyi and Muhammad Sani Umar, returned recently as visiting scholars. Three papers for this conference are written by Nigerian Northwestern graduates. In the past we have had long-term research programs to which senior Nigerian scholars have contributed, such as Anthony Asiwaju and Akin Mabogunje. And now we have a new fellowship program that has a Nigerian section. Individually, Nigeria's scholars have inspired our work and collaborated in our collective endeavours. So it gives us great pleasure to take this occasion to reaffirm our commitment to Nigeria.

OKIGBO'S VISION AND SCHOLARSHIP

The corpus of Okigbo's scholarly work is of intrinsic and continuing interest. It is not my place here to review it; that is best covered by those who knew him closely in Nigeria, and during the presentations of the conference. But I mention some of the ideas that were developed here in Evanston, or published here, including his dissertation, 'Capital Formation in a Developing Economy' (1956), and his first major book, *Nigerian Public Finance*, published by Northwestern University Press in 1965, as well as by Longman. In 1956, he traced the implications of the main sources of capital accumulation as being small-scale production and wages in an economy without a full menu of financial institutions to mobilize it. In 1965, he directed his attention to the national level, examining how 'Fiscal structure relates to the disposition of powers to raise revenue and incur expenditure between tiers of authority', and looking at what the history and alternative forms of these political dispositions augur for economic growth. Both family savings and national fiscal structure are perennial issues with respect to the mobilization of capital for development, and both topics are fraught with intellectual and political difficulties. But Okigbo approached both with detailed scholarship, clarity of analysis and exposition, and perhaps above all, thoughtful realism. How can I resist quoting to you, coming as I do from research on urban-rural relations, his blunt and unequivocal statement that 'the primary function of Nigerian agriculture should be to feed the population....?'

Okigbo's vision of the role of the state was based both on theory and on his own turbulent experience of Nigeria's postindependence politics. Neither ideologically for nor against state enterprise *per se*, as a nationalist he was surely a champion of an important economic role for the state and high levels of expertise and probity for its public servants. In his *Essays on the Public Philosophy of Development* he wrote: 'A Government that is too weak to attain its objectives in terms of welfare of the citizen through the exercise of powers over the private sector may not do that much better simply by substituting public for private ownership' (p.75). Does advocating a strong state necessarily mean advocating centralization? Doubtless he discussed such issues with Stolper, who wrote in *Planning without Facts* that 'only by decentralization can low skills find their niche in the productive process. Central control is not likely to create a place for them. It is more likely to inhibit their emergence...' (p12). In a later work, Okigbo writes of the 'architecture of our policies', evoking a considered and coherent assemblage that comes closer to Adibe's *'dirigiste'* model than Stolper's approach. One wonders still about the workable mix of intellectual clarity and popular participation, as the nation again struggles to define a workable democracy.

Doubtless such central questions were already present in Okigbo's earliest professional thinking. Also present very early on, would be his admiration for his brother's poetry. When we searched for a title for the workshop we thought of finding an apposite phrase in the poetry of Christopher Okigbo, one of Nigeria's most important poets. Provisionally we picked two promising phrases. But we felt, in the end, that his writing was too complex and allusional – to Igbo and classical mythology, to other modern poets such as Ezra Pound – to yield easily to the straightforward 'announcement' function we wanted it to serve. As Chinua Achebe said of him, 'he enjoyed getting to his destination through different routes'. So we chose something simple. But by the time we decided on a non-poetic title, we were already committed to the idea of reading some of his brother's poetry, as part of our tribute. So we asked a performance artist in our midst, David Donkor from Ghana who is a graduate student in performance studies, to read three of the sequence of poems published under the title *Limits*.

CONFERENCE THEMES

We were delighted with the acceptance of Ambassador Arthur Mbanefo, permanent representative of Nigeria to the United Nations, to deliver the keynote address. An accountant by profession, he trained in Britain, the United States and Nigeria, after which he served as a partner in the accountancy firm of Akintola Williams and Co. for 24 years, until 1986 when he founded his own firm. He has worked on financial aspects of the oil sector, aviation, insurance, motor vehicle manufacturing, banking, and many other components of the Nigerian private sector. At the same time he has served in the public domain: on a presidential commission on the National Electric Power Authority (NEPA), as pro-chancellor at three federal universities, on the States Creation, Local Government and Boundaries Adjustment Committee, and in many other capacities. In addition, he holds two important chieftaincy titles: one as successor to his late father as Odu of Onitsha as well as a Yoruba title at Ile-Ife. His career spans a wide spectrum of Nigerian public life.

What themes emerged from our discussions of the papers? My introduction can allude only briefly to a few striking points. First and most pervasively, the participants found the issues with which Okigbo had grappled to be still intensely relevant to Nigerian public life. Some of the younger participants had read his work for the first time, and found in it the persisting difficult challenges of, for example, finding economic regionalism attractive and important without being able to provide strong theoretical or empirical justification for it. Those who had served as advisors of one kind or another were deeply engaged by the problem of balancing one's own hope for the future with sober judgment about the means available, and of finding ways of serving the public interest even when both hope and integrity are betrayed. Elder statesmen had a rich terrain to look back on, to try to identify where different pathways might have been taken to better effect.

Dr. Sylvester Ugoh pointed out that Pius Okigbo was a *public official* as opposed to a *government official*, having never served in a ministerial role after the demise of Biafra. Others were sceptical that this protected his independence, and wondered about the fine line between formal autonomy and a kind of objectivity that ends up in complicity when it is likely from the outset that advice will be ignored. Yet others referred to the lack of consensus among the Nigerian elite, including its intellectuals, which detracts from the power of a principled individual stance. Some took a more institutional approach, while others were inclined to return to the issue of personal integrity and its challenges. The new democracy established in 1998 was already running up against chronic institutional weaknesses, so these discussions circled around various possibilities for ensuring greater accountability within and between strata in the political system. One contingent argued both positions: that there was no more important advice of integrity to give, contrary to Okigbo's own practice, and that was to drastically reduce the importance of the state in economic life, of advisors in policy formulation and of models from elsewhere (such as the European Union as the only successful model of regional integration).

By implication, we had returned to the greater pragmatic rigour of Stolper, the self-professed outsider to Nigerian political life. In the process, the question was raised of how ethnic leadership and ethnic agendas affect the status of those who would be public intellectuals. And more extremely, the point was raised that the only constraint on visionary leadership becoming sociopathic is the 'common sense shown by the majority of the people'. The formal sessions ended on the immediate issues of the present: the viability of the current Nigerian constitution, the advisability of a national conference, the travails of federalism everywhere in the world, and the critically important role of civil society. Informal discussions continued long after the final session. Indeed they will continue in smaller and more casual meetings amongst the participants, and in the activities of the Program of African Studies, long into the future.

ACKNOWLEDGEMENTS

We would like to note that the keynote address was supported by one of our treasured small endowment funds, given to the Program of African Studies by William B. Lloyd to support an annual lecture entitled the *Toward Freedom* Lecture, to be devoted to democracy and justice. Our keynote lecture for the conference is also our WBL/TF lecture for the academic year 2000–2001. We owe thanks to the Program of African Studies and Northwestern University for funding the conference; Akbar Virmani, then associate director, and the staff of the Program of African Studies who did all the organization; and the participants who provided inspiration and, in some cases, their own funding. This work was originally published in the Working Papers Series of the Program of African Studies. We thank Richard Joseph, the current director, for permission to publish this work in Nigeria. In Nigeria, we are grateful to the Centre for Social Science Research and Ford Foundation for funding the publication of this volume; Adigun Agbaje for his service as intermediary in the publication of this volume; and Mrs. Chinwe Adigwe, the deputy director, and Mr. Braimah Saibu, the production officer, at Ibadan University Press for their great assistance in making this work possible.

PART I: MEMOIRS AND TRIBUTES

1

THE MAN, DR. PIUS NWABUFO CHARLES OKIGBO

2001 Toward Freedom/William B. Lloyd Lecture and Keynote Address

Arthur C. I. Mbanefo, FCA, MFR

INTRODUCTION

I take this opportunity to thank Henry S. Bienen, Esq., the president of Northwestern University for his invitation to me to participate in this conference dedicated to an illustrious alumnus of the university and a great son of Africa, indeed of the world. I also wish to put on record my appreciation to all those who conceived the idea of dedicating this year's 'Toward Freedom/William B. Lloyd' lecture to Dr. Pius Nwabufo Charles Okigbo, in particular Professor Jane Guyer, head of the Program of African Studies, Northwestern University and her collaborators.

The conference that is scheduled for tomorrow, Saturday, June 9, 2001, has the general theme 'Vision and Policy in Nigerian Economics: The Legacy of Pius Okigbo'. It will discuss Okigbo's contributions to the evolution of the Nigerian state; economic policy and public finance in Nigeria and the African continent; and intellectuals, public leadership and civil society. For my address today, therefore, I have chosen to talk about the man, Pius Okigbo, in the hope that people who may not have known him in life would have an insight of who he was and perhaps why he is being so lavishly honoured by the Program of African Studies.

FAMILY

Dr. Pius Nwabufo Charles Okigbo, B.A. (Hons), B. Sc. Econ, LLB, D.Sc. Econ. (London). M.A. and Ph. D. (Northwestern), Commander of the Distinguished Order of the Niger (CON), Nigeria National Merit Award (NNMA), Nwanne Bu Ugwu, Eze Onu Nekwuluora and Ebekuodide I of Ojoto, Anambra State of Nigeria, was born on February 6, 1924 to the family of a pioneer Catholic schoolmaster, Chief James Okoye Okigbo. His ancestor, Chief Eze Okigbo, was famous for bringing education to the town of Ojoto. Pius was the second child of his mother. They were five children altogether. Today, there are only two survivors from that marriage, the only girls among the siblings.

EDUCATION

Pius had laid a very good foundation for his higher education at Christ the King College, Onitsha where he had a most brilliant academic career. In 1940, he passed the Cambridge School Certificate examination in Grade I with exemption from London matriculation. The following year, he enrolled in the Higher College, Yaba, Lagos for a diploma course in arts. This was the highest institution of learning then in Nigeria and only the best managed to get in. There he read Latin, Greek, history and English language and literature. Subsequently, he completed his diploma in 1943 at Achimota College, in the Gold Coast (now Ghana), because the Yaba Higher College campus in Lagos had been converted to a military base for the Royal West African Frontier Force as World War II raged. Pius returned to Onitsha in 1943 and started teaching at the Africa College. By sheer dedication and self-discipline, he started working for the intermediate examinations of B.A., B.Sc. and L.L.B. degrees of London University as an external student, learning through correspondence courses. He successfully completed the courses between 1944 and 1947. In 1946 he graduated B.A. Honours (history) with second class upper division. While working as an African development officer, he graduated, again by correspondence courses, B.Sc. Economics (1949) and LLB (1952), both of London University. These rare achievements most probably qualified him as the first Nigerian to earn three degrees from London University by correspondence as an external student.

Pius's greatest chance for the advancement of his quest for education and self-development came when, in 1952, he was awarded the fellowship of the Institute of International Education tenable at Northwestern University, Evanston, Illinois. During the five years he spent at Northwestern, he completed course requirements for two postgraduate degrees, the M.A. in 1954 and the Ph.D. in 1956. Propelling his unquenchable thirst for education and academic excellence were various scholarships and studentships, including the Schaefer fellowship in economics at Northwestern University (1953), a Carnegie fellowship in economics (1953-1954), a studentship at Nuffield College, Oxford, England (1954-1955, 1957-1958) and the American Philosophical Society postdoctoral fellowship also in Oxford (1957-1958). But his crowning moment came in 1982 when, at the age of 58, he obtained the D. Sc. (Economics) degree of London University by examination. This singular achievement put him in the list of the chosen few of six academic giants that have earned this degree by examination in the many years of existence of that university.

WORKING CAREER

In 1948, Dr. Pius Okigbo started his short but most eventful bureaucratic career in Aba, Eastern Nigeria as an African development officer, a senior service post until then reserved for white colonial officers. He subsequently left in 1952 on obtaining a scholarship award that brought him to Northwestern University in the same year. In his five years in the United States of America, he was able to bring himself to a level, that as an African, he could be appointed lecturer in top grade universities in North America and the United Kingdom during the preindependence period. From 1955 to 1957, he worked as a lecturer at Northwestern University, as a research associate in the University of Chicago, and in the summer of 1957, ended up as research associate at the University of Wyoming. In 1957-1958, he served as a lecturer in Oxford University during his postdoctoral fellowship there.

On his return to Nigeria in 1958, Pius was employed in the Eastern Nigeria civil service as permanent secretary (planning) and economic adviser of the premier. While in Oxford, Pius had, as a postdoctoral fellow, using mathematical models, created unavailable economic data for Nigeria. In recognition of this achievement, he was offered these high posts in the Eastern Nigeria government. Towards the end, in 1959, he was appointed economic adviser to the Prime Minister of the Federal Government of Nigeria, Sir Abubakar Tafawa Balewa. It was said that in economic matters, the prime minister was often ready to side with Dr. Okigbo against his cabinet. Needless to add, that the inroad of Pius into economic advisory work and planning meant the end of dependence of African countries on western foreign economists for advice.

Subsequently, Dr. Okigbo was appointed Nigeria's ambassador to the European Economic Community in Brussels in 1963, a post he held until the civil war started in 1967. Pius followed his fellow Igbos to the Republic of Biafra where he was appointed economic adviser to the new government.

The high points of his brief career in the civil service of various governments of Nigeria included the following:

1.   During his service in the Eastern Nigeria civil service, he joined Professor Wolfgang Stolper to prepare the first national development plan for Nigeria. Their singular effort was acclaimed as laying the foundation of Nigeria's postindependence prosperity. The plan was so well calculated and prepared that its targets were not only met but also in some cases exceeded. Whereas the planners had projected an average national growth rate of 5.1 percent per annum during the plan period, by 1965 a growth rate of 6.7 percent had been attained. In the same period capital formation rose from 12.2 percent in 1962 to 15 percent in 1965 and the ratio of investment to GDP went up from 9.8 percent to 12.1 percent. It is also acknowledged that the economy of the former Eastern Region was the fastest growing in the federal republic and, indeed, in the world as of 1966 when the democratic government of Nigeria was dismantled by a military coup d'état.

2.   As Nigeria's ambassador to the European Economic Community, Pius's economic prowess earned him respect from his associates and negotiating partners. He combined his clear understanding of the political economy and diplomacy to build a model of association between the EEC and Nigeria. He succeeded in negotiating favourable trading terms with his European hosts. Nigerian commodities were thus given special entry rights into Europe without compromising Nigeria's freedom in world trade. He also succeeded in obtaining exemptions from European customs and fiscal charges without Europe insisting on reciprocity.

3.   In the short-lived Republic of Biafra, he succeeded in helping with the establishment of the Central Bank of Biafra and produced the republic's currency. Before that, Nigeria's currency was used in Biafra, but he convinced the government that a truly independent nation must have its own currency.

4.   On the international plane, he served as a member of the committee for technical cooperation for Africa South of the Sahara (CCTA) from 1960 to 1965. In 1961 he became chairman of the United Nations panel of experts that planned the setting up of an African Development Bank (ADB), which still operates in the Ivory Coast where it is located. He was chairman of the ADB's Council of African Advisers from 1993 until his death. In 1962, he was appointed a member of the Kenya Fiscal Commission. In the same year he also served as a member of various international bodies, including the United Nations

Panel of Experts in the Institute of Economic Development for Africa, the External Advisory Board of the Organization for Economic Cooperation and Development Centre in Paris (1963-1966), and as the chairman of the Committee on Commodities, United Nations Conference for Trade and Development (UNCTAD), Geneva (1964-1966).

POST-CIVIL SERVICE CAREER

At the end of the Nigerian Civil War and the collapse of the Republic of Biafra in 1970, Pius was arrested and imprisoned for eighteen months in Enugu Prison for his role in Biafra. On his release from prison, he decided that his services were no longer welcome by the government of Nigeria. In 1971, he established a multisectoral consultancy company known as SKOUP and Company Limited. From the inception of the company to his demise in September 2000, Pius served as its managing director and chief executive officer. SKOUP was a pioneer consultancy firm of local experts involved in planning and project development; research that provided or generated data for planning and project development; the review, monitoring and assessing of programming impacts; and the provision of advisory services in diverse sectoral development programs in agriculture, forestry, natural resources, conservation, management, industry, engineering, research and development, education, transportation, etc. The staff included economists, accountants, engineers, agriculturists, chemists, sociologists, information management experts and others. This was a very successful firm whose services were sought after not only by private sector organizations but also the state and federal governments of Nigeria and international agencies.

Working out of government no doubt gave Dr. Okigbo the freedom he needed to engage in his hobby and life: economics. He was not a university don required to produce scholarly publications to rise to the top. Nevertheless, he wrote easily and extensively to put on record his views on diverse issues. In this regard there was no doubt that his major business interests might have suffered neglect. He was chairman of Bouygues, an international construction company, the Nigerian Tobacco Company, Torch Publishing Company, Magnum Trust Bank as well as a member of a host of companies, foundations and other institutions.

Despite his direct management and control of these various enterprises, Pius found time to serve on international and national commissions as chairman or as an invaluable member. Thus in 1976, he was the chairman of the Constitution Drafting Committee and the chairman of the subcommittee that worked on economics, finance and division of power. He also served as a member of the Constituent Assembly (1978) that approved the 1979 constitution and as chairman of the Presidential Commission on Revenue Allocation (1979–1980). An innovation he introduced to this very sensitive and delicate policy issue in Nigeria, which was to create the formula for the redistribution of Nigeria's income to the component governments (federal, state and local government), was to use primary school enrolment as a criterion for revenue allocation. During the Sani Abacha regime, he was chairman of the Panel of Inquiry into the Gulf War Oil Windfall, otherwise known as the Okigbo Inquiry into the Central Bank of Nigeria. Pius demonstrated tremendous courage and integrity when in his committee's report he categorically indicted the military government of the day for displaying a penchant for wasteful spending on projects that had little or no economic value. In 1996, he was the chairman of the committee that laid down the national policy on solid minerals development. Lastly, with the resumption of civilian democratic government in 1999 under President Olusegun Obasanjo, he was appointed as a special adviser on economic matters to the president, a position he held until his death.

At the international level, Dr. Pius Okigbo took active part in policy discussions for South-South development and cooperation. He was well known for his membership in the South Commission (1987–1990). From 1995 to the day he died, he served on the board of governors of the South Centre. He also served as a member of the United Nations Panel of Experts on the Reform of the Tax System in the Third World in 1989. He served in so many other capacities that I need not list all of them here.

OKIGBO'S ECONOMICS
Being independent of government service helped Pius to do what he loved doing best: finding the right path for Nigerian development. His concern centred on the phasing of public initiatives and the structuring of individual policies and programs. Naturally, it was only being free of government requirements and entanglements that he could make a global search for development options, comparing plans in different parts of the globe like India, the Soviet Union, Mexico and Malaysia, to mention only a few.

A strong belief in the development of human capital guided Pius's economic thinking. He committed himself to working for the benefit of his fellow men and women. He subscribed to the school of thought that 'knowledge that is not at the service of society is a waste'. According to his way of thinking, the core essence of economics is about ordinary people and so he embraced what we may call here the humanistic brand of economics. Opining that the difference between industrialized nations and developing ones is the difference in the quality of their human resources, he asserted that the most important agent of development is man not mineral deposits, for man assigns value to mineral resources. Without man, therefore, no mineral has any value.

Moreover, when resources are spent on education, this creates a tremendous asset for humanity, and thus he strongly advocated that the profits of Nigeria's considerable national resources be expended on the education and welfare of its people. So it is not surprising that the report of the South Commission, of which he was an invaluable member, stressed that 'man is both the means and the end of development'.

Dr. Okigbo's theory differed from the economics of the International Monetary Fund, the World Bank, the Economic Commission for Africa and even the Federal Government of Nigeria on what it meant to be poor and how to end poverty. He agreed that food production could well be the leading sector to take Nigeria out of her troubles. He wondered why Operation Feed the Nation, the Green Revolution and the River Basin Development Authorities did not change the lot of our people. He concluded that they failed because they did not simultaneously pursue a manufacturing program for agricultural equipment and inputs. Consequently, foreign exchange availability became a key factor against the success of these policies. Also, the budgetary allocation to carry out these schemes never trickled down to the peasant communities upon whom the heavy burden of producing food for the nation rested. In addition, the absence of social policy to liberate the energies and the marginalization of rural communities frustrated the success of the programs.

Another example of Dr. Okigbo's vision and contribution to Nigeria economic thought concerned privatization. In principle, Pius agreed with the idea of privatization but disagreed with the policy if it resulted in the freeing of the economy from government intervention or conceding ownership to powerful multinational investors. He thought that such a situation would exacerbate already existing global inequalities. If it meant the transfer of ownership and management from public to private managers, the question then arose: Where would the expert private managers come from? For privatization to be effective, he concluded, it must be accompanied by widening and deepening the production base and by planned expansion of managerial skills. Thus, privatization must involve the whole economy and should not be limited to specific enterprises. The whole program must be monitored and supervised to ensure that vulnerable groups were not deprived of opportunities for their own self-improvement.

Pius found the development taking place among the Asian Tigers exciting, particularly when compared with the sad records of perspectives in sub-Saharan Africa. Deeply interested in mathematical modelling and fascinated by the idea of catastrophe theories as a possible explanatory hypothesis of economic and political failures in Africa, Pius was a prodigious writer. He published seven books, about eighty scholarly articles and other collaborative publications. In addition, he participated in the drafting of reports of the many panels, committees and commissions on which he had served. He was a man imbued with genuine concern for the common man; his forte was economic planning for the eradication of poverty and inequity, especially in the third world. In several of his writings and public lectures, he unambiguously identified corruption and mismanagement of state resources as major factors hindering the growth of third world economies. Economics was his life. His pursuit for academic excellence was insatiable. He was fully committed to the pursuit of ideas and he wrote until his last days; he was never satisfied until he had attained the perfection for which he aimed; he brought to his writings all the knowledge he had derived from history, philosophy, politics, law, mathematics and many other disciplines. He had computed and refined the tables used in his work on the Nigerian debt problem, a subject that engaged him extensively throughout his life. This was his last work, which he had hoped to publish in mid-September 2000.

CONTRIBUTION TO PUBLIC DEBATE

Pius delighted Nigerian intellectuals and others by his fearlessness in speaking his mind on government policy and all manner of economic, political, social and cultural issues. He was not a sycophant and did not pander to any government or group. In his paper aptly titled, 'The Grammar of the Future', Pius predicted that science is the language of the future and technology its grammar. He attempted to persuade Nigerians to appreciate the role of science and technology in future development. In a 1993 keynote address at a conference on energy and development, he carefully and systematically debunked all the self-serving arguments used to explain the unsatisfactory state of the Nigerian energy sector. His assertions in that paper remain valid today as the Nigerian energy sector lies prostrate and comatose. On the occasion of receiving an honorary degree from the University of Lagos, he gave a lecture, titled 'Crises in the Temple', in which he admonished the university for the decline in our educational institutions. Condemning the nefarious influence of money on academics, he remarked that about eighty percent of the honorary doctorate degrees awarded by Nigerian universities went to people with little or no education but who were ready to 'settle' the university authorities with their wealth.

To show the range of Pius's views on issues that have engaged Nigerians in continuous debate for the latter half of the twentieth century, I quote from his writing on three subjects: religion, ethnicity and public leadership. On religion, he contended that:

The existence of multiple religions does not by itself create a special problem; it does so only where it is used as basis for a contest for the control of the state or when it is used to deal with other peoples classified as enemies. The state must provide security for its citizens to worship whatever god they please in whatever form they choose so long as they do not trample on the rights of other citizens.

This was long before the attempts to introduce the Sharia Law in parts of Nigeria and the bitter consequences of its application in many parts of the country. How right he was in his assertion!

On ethnicity, he wrote:

> The mere existence of the nation does not guarantee unity; unity can only be created and made by its members. Any unity achieved without the willing assent of the nationalities in the system cannot persist... Any unity that is contrived or imposed becomes in the words of Harold Laski's quaint phrase, 'unity of the cannibal and his victim'...to weld together the strands of the society from communal to ethnic requires cooperation of all units that is federal and not imperial in character.

And on the importance of committed public leadership, he contended that:

> The leader must not merely administer the creed of his time, he must be an age or two ahead of his time; must think not only of the day but of the morrow otherwise even if he is a first rate man he would be propagating the creed of a second rate man. He must be able to express in grand and articulate manner the yearnings and aspirations of his people and give them a vision and a passion that will suffuse everyone and everything around him: that Nigeria's First Magistrate (that is the President) has therefore two courses of action to choose from either to subscribe to the belief that progress is inevitable and so follow either the example of an Irish Bishop reputed to have said to his congregation: 'Brethren, here indeed is a great difficulty. Let us look it firmly in the face and then pass on'.

> Or accept the challenge facing his leadership and decide to be more aggressive by adopting the route defined by Confucius when he said 'Taking the bull by the horns always yields results even if it is the bull that gets the results'. However, the President having chosen the option prescribed by Confucius, it is up to us Nigerians to ensure that it is not the bull that gets the results and that the President he heartened and encouraged by modification and adaptation of the famous statement by the

Russian philosopher Ostrogovsky to wit: 'God himself takes care of infants and lunatic'.

THE HUMAN PIUS

The man Pius Nwabufo Charles Okigbo cannot be understood nor fully appreciated if we concentrate only on his life as an economist and an intellectual. He fits squarely the legend of the African elephant about which it is said contains the meat of all the other animals in the world. Consequently, one was supposed to find in the elephant any kind of meat that one desired. We can only properly visualize the man from all the diverse viewpoints of his incredibly full life as a professional, an academic, a development economist, a business tycoon, a political analyst, a philanthropist, a sage, a wit, a socioculturist at local, national and international levels. Above all, he was a family man.

A very humble, personable and affectionate man, Pius was highly regarded and respected by all. As the saying goes, Pius took his work very seriously, but like many a genius of his class he never took himself seriously. Thus, he was able to adjust to any situation in which he found himself without fuss. He was very witty and entertaining and had the knack for keeping his friends fully engaged humorously with the many funny stories he skilfully chose to fit every occasion.

Pius was unaffected in behaviour or personality by success or fame. Trying to describe his maturity and relaxed confidence brings to mind a description of the great jazz musician Dizzy Gillespie that I once read: 'He never took advantage of who he was, and he never acted like a star. I don't know how stars get from here to there, but Dizzy walked down the street'. Pius surely did walk down the street! Indeed, throughout his years of success and public acclaim he managed to remain his good self, unpretentious, humorous, kindly and down-to-earth. He was much more concerned with the achievement of results than with getting credit for the results. The struggles of the young and the disadvantaged in society moved him more than did the caprice and favours of the great and famous. He never forgot his origins and where he came from. He was overwhelmed with unresolved human problems of his world and the world around him.

Dr. Okigbo was said to write economics with the same ease with which he played the piano, with flourishes of graceful notes and wayward harmonies. On a humorous side, he never stopped admiring a fellow student at Northwestern University who started a doctoral dissertation on packaging with what was really a joke – a discussion of mummification in ancient Egypt. He was an unusual man. Glowing tributes have been paid to his sparkling humour and his great intellect. In his lifetime he was known to be very charitable, as manifested by the number of underprivileged persons he had helped through school, loaned money, bailed out of financial and other difficulties, and assisted in getting employment, without making an issue about it. He donated freely to charitable causes and development projects.

Pius was never known to be a card-carrying political party member, but it was generally acknowledged that he wielded considerable influence in the Nigerian political arena. Described by many as a detribalized patriot, he was motivated in his political leanings by the need for justice, fair play and equity. During the Abacha transition period and after, he became a very prominent member of Ohaneze Ndigbo, a pan-Igbo organization that is committed to ensuring that the rights of the Igbos in Nigeria were fully recognized and met. He also believed and advocated the right of the Igbos to play a role that would ensure their relevance in the political equation of Nigeria.

Not only was Pius respected and revered in urban Nigeria, Africa and the world, he was loved, respected and deeply appreciated by the people of his hometown, Ojoto, for despite his acquired education, success and cosmopolitan outlook, he remained very closely linked with his roots. All and sundry accepted him as a patriotic son of Ojoto. In his village Ire, Ojoto he created the Ire Higher Education Foundation for the award of scholarships to sons of Ire village who gained admission to universities, but were adjudged unable to pay the fees. Significantly, in a country where all types of chieftaincy titles were often awarded to non-indigenes of towns, Pius only held titles bestowed on him in his hometown, Ojoto. Although he was not engaged in local town politics, he always succeeded in playing roles that insured that peace and tranquillity reigned all the time in Ojoto. For all these and more, he was honoured with the title of Ebukuedike I of Ojoto.

Pius participated actively in many professional societies and associations. These included the Royal Economic Society of the United Kingdom, the American Economic Society, the International Association for Research in Income and Wealth, the International Institute of Public Finance, the American National Register of Mathematical Sciences, the Nigerian Economic Society (of which he was a former president and the first fellow), the International Association for Mathematical Modelling, the Association for Comparative Economic Studies and the Nigerian Institute of Management. In acknowledgement of the achievements of this great man the following honours and honorary degrees were bestowed on him: Conmander of the Distinguished Order of the Niger (CON) (1977); National Order of Merit (NOM) (1983); International Order of Merit (IOM) (1992); Zik's Prize for Leadership in Africa (1996); Honorary L.L.D., University of Nigeria, Nsukka; Honorary D. Litt., Ahmadu Bello University, Zaria; Honorary D. Litt., Federal University of Technology, Owerri; Honorary D.Sc. University of Lagos, Lagos; and Honorary D. Litt., Nnamdi Azikiwe University, Awka.

In his leisure hours, Pius was a gifted chess player who always kept his strategies close to his heart. Opponents who mistook his caution for cowardice often did so at their peril. He was the national chess champion for many years.

Last, but not least, Pius was a happily married man. His love and affection for his wife and children lasted until his last day. He often shared his humorous jokes with his grown-up children.

CONCLUSION

In bringing this address to a close, let me once again thank this university and the Program of African Studies in particular for the honour they have done my country man, an alumnus and former faculty member. This singular gesture on your part would tend to disprove Shakespeare's assertion that 'the good is often interred with the bones'. In the life of Pius, merit and hard work are today rewarded. It is obvious that his pioneering role in promoting developmental economic philosophy in Nigeria and Africa, nay in all developing countries, cannot be forgotten in a hurry.

2

DEVELOPMENT PLANNING IN NIGERIA: A MEMOIR[1]

Wolfgang F. Stolper

My terms of reference for this contribution have been very generous and I am grateful for this. To start with: it is fitting that Northwestern University honours Pius Okigbo, its first African Ph.D. in economics. There is no question that Pius was a highly intelligent and very well trained economist in the classical tradition. I stress 'classical', because I myself was Schumpeter-trained and, as a Schumpeterian, had a basically different way to look at development problems, in fact a view of economics, which put development and growth – I leave both terms undefined at least for the present – at the centre of analysis. The central point of the Schumpeterian analysis is that the future is in principle unknowable, and that decisions which, when originally made, were perfectly rational and correct, may and do *become* wrong. This does not prevent different observers from having slightly better noses for the immediate future, but it requires constant attention and sensitivities to what is going on in the economy and makes purely formulaic approaches impossible.

---

[1] Professor Stolper died during the preparation of this volume on April 1, 2002, six weeks before his 90th birthday. He kept a diary of his stay in Nigeria, now published as *Inside Independent Nigeria: Diaries of Wolfgang Stolper, 1960–1962* (coedited by Stolper and Clive S. Gray, 2003), which provides rich detail about Nigeria at that time and about the daily work of an economic advisor. In view of the personal contribution it makes to Nigerian policy history, the editors thought it suitable to add explanations of the careers of those to whom he refers only by name. These annotations are therefore the responsibility of the editors and not the author of the paper. For a series of memoirs about Stolper, see *ISS Forum: The Newsletter of the International Joseph A. Schumpeter Society*, no.7, August 2002.

But these matters are swamped by the problem of being an economic advisor. Both the native son and the outsider must gain the confidence of the people whom he is called to advise. The outsider has, as a rule one advantage: he can quit. I, at least, had this advantage. My career was determined by the academic side of my life. 'You want me to stay, I'll stay. You want me to leave, I go home'. Of course, there are outsiders who are professional advisors, but if they were any good, they would have the backing of their institutional employers. They would have to be either freelance advisors, or be willing to stay under any circumstances for some reasons of their own.

But even the insider, if he were any good academically, as Pius certainly was, would have a choice. I am sure that Pius could have found an academic position in the West or a position with an international organization, as for example, Godfrey Lardner[2] did. I myself, when I was the director of the Center for Economic Development (CRED) at the University of Michigan, did invite Ojetunji Aboyade, who was, I believe, the first African economist to teach the course on economic development, and I know that, had he decided to stay, I could have found the financing for him.[3] I am aware that it is never easy for anyone to leave his familiar surroundings, and to emigrate. I was, after all, forced by Hitler to undergo this experience, and that everything turned out well was neither foreseeable nor foreseen.

But there are two other problems that any advisor has. No advisor can expect that all his advice will be taken. Politics requires compromises. And the advisor cannot always know what his minister has to deal with. But there are some matters that he must decide he cannot support and which are reasons for resigning. In my case, I was determined not to support exchange controls or even standby legislation in case it might become necessary,

---

[1] Godfrey E. A. Lardner was a Sierra Leonean who joined the staff of the United Nations. He served as head of the transport and communications Division of the Economic Commission of Africa in the early 1970s (Anonymous 1975).

[2] Ojetunji Aboyade (1931–1994) strongly believed that it was the duty of Nigerian intellectuals to contribute to nation building and shaping continental African policy. He was one of the founders of the department of economics at the University of Ibadan in 1960. In 1975, he reluctantly accepted appointment as vice-chancellor of the University of Ife (now Obafemi Awolowo University), an experience that confirmed his disinclination to seek further high office. However, he believed that it was important to take part in shaping national economic policy, and consequently served in various advisory capacities, including chairman of the Presidential Advisory Committee during the regime of General Ibrahim Babangida. He was also a member of the Council of African Advisers at the World Bank and a consultant to the United Nations Development Program, various bilateral agencies and the African Capacity Building Foundation, based in Harare, Zimbabwe (Mabogunje 2000, 17–20).

which the Indian advisor to the prime minister wanted.[4] This hostility was not based on some abstract principle, but on an observation: exchange controls permitted the rich and powerful to transfer their capital abroad on, for them, exceedingly favourable terms. Just as I found Kaldor[5], who thought most subsidies were transferred from the poor to the poor, to be wrong. Indeed, I found them to be mostly subsidies from the poor to the rich.

This problem is actually comparatively simple. Much more difficult is the fact that advice given at a particular moment might prevent great harm, while given at another moment might at best be simply irrelevant. I found that I was very good at preventing harm, but found it difficult to undo harm, once it had occurred. This might have been partly a personal failing. But it surely was also much more. Real time runs only in one direction. Most of the time you simply cannot pretend that a decision made can simply be reversed. You deal with what Brian Arthur has established to be path dependence. (I am discussing here the comparatively short-term framework within which advisors work.) But it is enough to discuss the few major problems of an advisor and it is time to turn to the actual problem which in due time landed me in Nigeria, of which collaboration with Pius Okigbo turned out to be a part, and not always a happy or fruitful part.

My interest in economic development started with a study of the then still communist East Germany. It started with developing a reasonably trustworthy database. This in turn involved sifting literally several cubic meters of material, which was more or less successfully done with the help of the now retired Professor Rolf Richter. A manuscript was sent for criticism to a person in East Berlin, who declined to make any official comments. However, I was told by the pseudonymous (if I may be permitted to coin such a word) Germanicus in the Foreign Office in London that the fact that I had developed such a database led to the publication of the first Statistical Abstract of the German Democratic Republic (GDR) (the official name of East Germany). There were two official reviews of my book. The Central

---

[1] Sir Abubakar Tafawa Balewa (1912–1966) served as Nigeria's first federal prime minister. A moderate politician, he unsuccessfully tried to balance the ideological and ethnic tensions that split the newly independent nation. Southerners believed him to be a pawn of the Sardauna of Sokoto. He was assassinated in the first military coup d'état (Clark 1991).

[2] Nicholas Kaldor (1908–1986) was one of the founders and foremost members of the Cambridge school of economists in the twentieth century. He made important contributions to the theories of equilibrium, the firm, capital, growth and welfare economics. After World War II, he turned to development theory, serving as advisor to the newly independent governments of India and Ceylon (now Sri Lanka). His ideas on development are outlined in *Strategic Factors in Economic Development* (1967) and *Economics without Equilibrium* (1985) (New School 2002).

Intelligence Agency (CIA) thought my conclusions to be too pessimistic. As it happened the CIA was wrong; I was not pessimistic enough. I also saw an internal East German review that thought my book to be fair and believed that it underestimated the achievements of the GDR. When I later met the author of the review at an international conference, he startled me by expressing an admiration for my courage! I thought I had just described the utter silliness of East German planning methods, a silliness *from their own standpoint*, and the fact that an industry-by-industry comparison with the Federal German Republic showed a hopeless failure. My 'courage' in the eyes of my East German colleague consisted in the fact that I had pointed out that the GDR was not about to collapse. The reason why I even mention this intellectual effort is that it turned out to be useful in Nigeria, when confronted by, among others, Sam Aluko, who insisted that capitalism was dead and the soviet countries were obviously superior.[6] My response at the time was that I was not sure whether capitalism was dead or not, but that it, in fact, was feeding the rest of the world including the communist countries.

Having investigated growth and development under a communist sign, I wanted to investigate growth in Africa. Basically, I wanted to see with my own eyes how a modern economy arose. Now obviously, the British, the French, the Germans, the Italians and the Belgians had been in Africa for some time, so some development had already taken place. Still, I was curious. I suggested at the Massachusetts Institute of Technology (MIT), specifically to Max Millikan,[7] who had invited me to do the East German study,

---

[1] Adepoju Samuel Aluko (b.1929), an economist renowned for independent thinking and fearless outspokenness, has consistently advocated that economic management should be based on public-private collaboration rather than the domination of the free market trade in the private sector. After an academic career in the University of Nigeria, Nsukka (1956–1966) and the University of Ife (1967), he taught at the Massachusetts Institute of Technology, the University of Birmingham, England and Harvard University. By 1980, he had returned to Nigeria and became the economic adviser to the Ondo State government under the leadership of Governor Adekunle Ajasin. He also worked with other ideologues to draft the economic blueprint of the United Party of Nigeria. Although he accepted public appointments under both civilian and military governments, he nevertheless refused to follow government dictates or countenance corrupt practices by government officials, no matter who they were, whether Obafemi Awolowo or General Sani Abacha (Adekanmbi 2000, 79–80).

[7] Max Franklin Millikan (1913–1969) had served as assistant director of the Central Intelligence Agency briefly from 1951 to 1952, and as a member of the Presidential Task Force for Aid in 1961. He coedited several works relating to foreign policy and economic development, including *A Proposal: Key to an Effective Foreign Policy* (1957, coedited with W.W. Rostow); *No Easy Harvest: The Dilemma of Agriculture in Underdeveloped Countries* (1967, coedited with David Hapgood); and *The Global Partnership: International Agencies and Economic Development* (1968, coedited with Richard N. Gardner).

that it was obvious that African countries would become independent as the colonial era was about to end, and that perhaps we might be prepared to deal with such a situation before it actually arose. MIT had thought about this already, so no great persuasion was necessary. So MIT arranged for me to go to Europe and visit colonial offices in London, Paris and Brussels, and to talk with people such as Dame Margery Perham[8] and Phyllis Deane.[9] Everybody received me graciously. I explained that I knew nothing, which was the literal truth, and hoped for enlightenment from them.

I did get much enlightenment, but also much information that later turned out to be totally useless. Much of the information concerned problems of stabilizing the labour force, which was a specific problem for the South African gold mines. Then, as at present, South Africa dominated much of the efforts of American policy. It is true that Senegal and Mali were also mentioned, and Senegal was a slaving port, but the ancestors of Secretary of State Colin Powell surely did not come from any of those places – they came from the Slave Coast, from West Africa. If Nigeria was mentioned, it was as a supplier of oil.

In any case, I returned from Europe totally frustrated, because I had not succeeded in setting foot in Africa. I collected what statistical material was available, I sent it to Phyllis Deane for criticism and suggestions, but I knew that the meaning of the data really eluded me. Upon my return to the University of Michigan, I talked with Gardner Ackley, the chairman of the department at the time, and got his promise of another leave if an opportunity arose to go to Africa to rescue what I felt was a lost year.[10] I was quite conscious that statistics and facts are not necessarily the same thing. Hence the name of my book, written after the Nigerian stint: *Planning without Facts*.

This opportunity arose almost immediately. I got an inquiry from the Harvard Advisory Service whether I would be interested in an advisory posi-

---

[8] Margery Freda Perham (1895–1982) was then one of the leading authorities on Nigerian colonial administration and political policy. Her work, *Native Administration in Nigeria* (1937, reprinted 1962), had been a primary reference for colonial officers serving in Nigeria (Kirk-Greene 1982).

[9] Phyllis Mary Deane (b.1918) is an economic historian who spent most of the 1950s and 1960s working in the field of national accounting, first developing a system of regional accounts for the United Kingdom and then advising on how this system could be applied to developing countries (Blaug 1999).

[10] H. Gardner Ackley (1915–1998) was chair of the department of economics at the University of Michigan from 1954 to 1960. Beyond the academy, he played a substantial role in American policy, serving as first a member and then the chair of the Presidential Council of Economic Advisers under Presidents John F. Kennedy and Lyndon B. Johnson. A man of strong principles, he openly supported academics under attack by the House Un-American Activities Committee during the 1950s (Friedman 1998).

tion in Nigeria. I went to Harvard to talk with the gentleman who had suggested me for the job, (and who later became President John F. Kennedy's chief of the bureau of the budget and the director of the United States Agency for International Development (USAID) It seems that the Nigerians had talked with the Pakistanis, who told them of the wonderful job that Harvard had done. I on my part had never worked for any government, domestic or foreign, and wanted assurance that I would be able to make a satisfactory job in an advisory position. Harvard promised to get me a good assistant with experience in manoeuvring in a governmental bureaucracy. And so it was agreed that I would go to as-yet colonial Nigeria for a few months to see whether I would like to accept an advisory position and whether the Nigerians would be ready to accept me. The Ford Foundation was ready to finance the enterprise.

I returned to Michigan to teach one semester, find replacements for me while I was gone, and prepare myself for a return to Lagos. Kingsley, the Ford Foundation representative in Lagos, who was to become a good friend, told me later, that when asked whether he would accept me, he wired back: 'Never heard of the guy, but if he is warm and breathes, send him'. My replacements were Just Faaland[11] from Bergen, Norway and Ian Stewart from Edinburgh, Scotland, who had worked with Pius Okigbo on the Nigerian national accounts and who spoke very highly of Pius, both of his technical competence and of his pleasant personality. So I was looking forward to meeting him very much.

The British arranged a thorough trip of Nigeria by plane and railroad, arranging interviews with Britons and Africans, who would answer my questions of what they were doing, how they were organized, how they saw their problems, and what they thought had to be done. It seems that this procedure went very well. While I knew nothing about Nigeria, I did know how to ask questions, and the manner of my asking made the interviewees aware that they really knew a lot more than they had realized, which naturally pleased them. The British had told me that they did not want someone who would tell other people what to do. They were desperate for people who would actually do the work. Would I be willing actually to be a working stiff? I thought that this would be just fine. It was this fact that would lead to some difficulties with Pius. He did not particularly like that I would be so directly involved with the planning work. And his idea of an economic adviser was:

---

[11] Just Faaland coauthored several works on the political economy of developing nations, including Tanzania, Kenya, Uganda, Bangladesh and Malaysia (Faaland and Dahl, 1968a, 1968b, 1968c; see also Faaland and Parkinson 1986).

'I don't like what you have brought me. Do it again, and see me then', or so I was told.

I have told how I approached my work in general terms in my book, *Planning without Facts*, avoiding references to personalities and day-to-day operations. I had been privy to much internal knowledge and wanted to avoid any direct reference to this. My book appeared in 1966. But, of course, the real work was done in day-to-day operations, with constant fights, successes and failures. I do not remember when I first met Pius. By the time I returned to Nigeria the country had become independent, but the British tradition was still strong. My first stop was in London where I got strong briefings and enthusiastic reports about Nigeria, and then I stopped in Rome, where I also consulted with the Food and Agricultural Organization (FAO). The Nigerian civil servants whom I met in Rome were themselves feeling their way, when they asked my advice, and at the FAO I got a briefing of their idea for farm settlements, which seemed ingenious and correct.

Once in Nigeria, I rapidly changed my mind. The farm settlements were far too expensive, which prevented them from being imitated, and they asked nothing from the intended settlers. The settlements were particularly obnoxious in the Eastern Region, where land was scarce and perfectly good farmers had to be displaced from their land to make room for fewer and less productive settlers. I do not know what Pius did or did not do in this case, but I suspect that in this particular case there was nothing he could have done. When I pointed out that at the end of the Second World War, no student could study at the University of Berlin who had not helped with cleaning up the rubble and helped rebuild it, this idea was dismissed as insulting to the sovereign nation of Nigeria. The settlers expected to have everything done for them and to be put into a position where they could tell some underlings what to do. I was willing to allow one to be constructed *au fond perdu* to see what could be learned. The major opposition to my arguments came from the Indian advisor to the prime minister, who in general turned out to be my main problem.

At that time, Nigeria was still divided into three regions, the North being mostly Muslim, but with strong Christian and pagan parts, the West being dominated by Yorubas, who were roughly half Christian and half Muslim, but with significant numbers of practitioners of traditional religion, and the Eastern Region, which was dominated by Igbos, but with substantial minority tribes such as Ibibios and Ijaws.

At first, my ministers changed several times, as did my permanent secretaries. Eventually I got my final minister, Waziri Ibrahim, who was totally accessible, interested and who backed me fully.[12] The difficulties I had with him were only that he tried to do things, which, while sensible, were not within the competence of our ministry. Eventually, I also got my first African permanent secretary, Godfrey Lardner. He had a reputation as being fiercely anti-white. I well remember my first meeting with him. I had been in a meeting with the permanent secretary of finance, the governor of the central bank and the Indian advisor to the prime minister about the safe amount of inflationary financing, and I had lost. (I was strongly anti-inflationary). I also did not appreciate it that the Indian played on the fact that he was brown and I was white. So I was in a foul mood when I got back to my office, where my deputy Lyle Hansen[13] had been briefing Lardner about what we had been doing. I remember this meeting very well. I told Lardner fiercely: 'If you think that I will pander to your nationalistic prejudices, you can think again!' To my surprise, Lardner stretched out his hand and said, 'I know that I have this reputation of being anti-white, but I am making my distinctions'.

All the problems that arose between Pius and myself stemmed from the fact that I became a *de facto* associate permanent secretary, in charge of discussing in detail and coordinating the federal and regional plans, with the full backing of my minister and my permanent secretary. Pius was the senior civil servant in charge of Eastern Region plans. There is no point in going into many details. I had the full backing of the permanent secretary of finance, a highly able Englishman, a highly decorated wing commander in the Royal Air Force, who was half German, but refused to speak a word of German after Hitler. I was consulted on the budget speech. The usual idea that finance is a 'no-ministry' and that development is a 'yes-ministry' was certainly not true in this case. It was myself, as much as anyone, who urged restraints on spending. My chief enemy was the Indian advisor whom I found totally wrong as well as totally untrustworthy, to the extent, that at the end I refused to meet with him except in the presence of another senior civil servant.

[12] After a career with United Africa Company of Nigeria Limited, Alhaji Waziri Ibrahim (1926–1992) became a NPC leader in northeastern Nigeria. Two years after independence, he was first appointed minister for health and then minister for economic development. During the transition to civilian rule in the late 1970s, he became the chairman of the Great Nigeria's People's Party (GNPP), and stood as its presidential candidate in the elections of 1979 and 1983. He was also chairman of the Herwa group of companies and the director of Beecham Nigeria Ltd. (Anyaegbunam 1992).

[13] Lyle Macdonald Hansen (b.1926) served as economic adviser to the Federal Ministry of Economic Planning in Nigeria from 1960 to 1963. Thereafter he was posted as senior economist to the African department of the International Bank for Reconstruction and Development (IBRD) where he remained until 1974 (*Who's Who in the United Nations and Related Agencies* 1975).

The problem with Pius was that he always tried to find out which way the wind was blowing, who seemed to be in power and who seemed to be making the important decisions. In a meeting of the joint economic committee, he changed his backing when the Indian seemed to be ahead. One exchange between us when he brought me some lousy stuff was literally:

'Pius, What am I supposed to do with this junk?', I asked.
'Wolf, if you were not older than I am, I would hit you', he replied.
'Go right ahead, but get me something I can use', I retorted.

In fact, I considered this to be a sign of excellent personal relations between us – that we could talk to each other like that. But I found it more serious that, when his good advice to his minister was first taken and then abandoned after the minister got cold feet, Pius refused to fight for his original good advice. There were other instances, where I could be helpful to him. I once got a phone call from him that his beautiful Congolese and American (I believe) wife had trouble being admitted to Nigeria, so I went dutifully over to the ministry of foreign affairs, to arrange for her re-entry to Nigeria.

The fact was that I worked 12–16 hours every day, except Sunday, which I used to write a detailed and rather indiscreet report to my wife about my activities and my judgements of persons (a diary which is about to be published). I conked out after about three weeks, when I got an assignment in the 'bush'. Driving was so dangerous that it was the only thing that really took my mind off my work. But there was also method in my madness. I had to see with my own eyes what was going on in the bush; I had to learn as much as I could about local cultures and habits. I did sleep in African huts and I went up to Lake Chad at the end of the rainy season. Of course, the regional planners did not as a rule appreciate my unauthorized visits, which they interpreted as my spying on them. When I got to Lake Chad – my most adventurous trip – I found out that the Food and Agricultural Organization (FAO) team, which had written a report on Lake Chad fishing, had never visited the area. I simply did not trust most of my fellow planners, who were too much concerned with personal comfort to go into the bush. This was certainly true for the Indian advisor. Pius, of course, did not have to do what I had to, because he was a local boy. Nevertheless, he tended to dislike my boy-scout-like behaviour that, despite my fifty years of age, I thoroughly enjoyed.

I do not wish to be too hard on Pius. Of course, I had always the option of going home to my academic place. Pius had to stay and to survive in a politically tricky environment in situations that I could not always understand. But even when the political situation had not deteriorated, Pius preferred to spend his time with his beloved *National Accounts*. When the FAO heard of my severe criticisms, they wanted me to come to Rome for a discussion. I declined because I simply could not take the time off from my work. I believe Pius went.

At the end, I had some triumphs, but they did not involve Pius, with whom relations remained friendly and, I believe, mutually appreciative. My difficulties always and invariably stemmed from the Indian advisor, and occasionally from Lyle Hansen, who fancied himself a politically sophisticated person, but whose knowledge all came from books, while I had a very solid political education. My father had been a member of the Reichstag and I myself had not only been constantly informed about what went on politically, but had been actively engaged in anti-Nazi student politics.

When the Indian double-crossing continued, I went on to see Stanley Wey, the prime minister's permanent secretary.[14] He apologized that he was unaware of the situation, pointing to a pile of documents on his desk. He not only backed me completely, but also invited me to come to the meeting of the second highest political level. The highest level was the meeting of the four prime ministers with no one else present. The second highest level was the meeting of the prime ministers with their advisors. While I was at first waiting outside the meeting room, Wey came out and asked me in. It was the first time that I actually saw the Sardauna[15] and his top advisor, both very impressive persons with strong, intelligent faces. The Indian advisor was asked some sharp questions, which he answered in rather silly ways. He had asked me originally to write some flowery stuff in the plan that he felt to be

[14] Stanley Olabode Wey (b.1923) served as secretary to the prime minister and council of ministers from 1961 to 1966. After the military overthrew the civilian government, he continued in government service, serving as secretary to the federal military government and head of service in 1966, and thereafter as commissioner on special duty in the Cabinet Office, Lagos; and as sole commissioner of the produce evacuation with federal emergency (war) power via the Nigerian Produce Marketing Company from 1967 to 1970. He retired from government service in 1973. Like Okigbo, he then turned to a distinguished career as a businessman and public intellectual. Among his many activities, he served a five-year period as the executive administrative director of Paterson Zochonis Nigeria Limited (1973–1978) and authored many publications on policy (Makinde 2001, 1366).

[15] At the time, the Sardauna was Sir Ahmadu Bello (1909–1966), the great-great-grandson of the founder of the Sokoto Caliphate, Shehu Usman dan Fodio. In 1939, he was installed as the Sardauna of Sokoto, thus becoming the most important Muslim traditional leader in northwestern Nigeria. He entered the national political arena in early 1950s when he was elected to a seat in the Northern Regional House of Assembly. Cofounder of the Northern People's Congress, he led the Northern Region government into self-government in 1953 and independence in 1960. His political career was terminated by assassination on January 15, 1966 during the first military coup d'état (Paden 1986).

elevating, I suppose. I had refused, suggesting that he might write it himself. I did not understand how they had spotted the sentences, but I confess that I thoroughly enjoyed his discomfort. Wey asked me whether I wanted to say something, which I declined to do. I confess also that I was totally confused by the obvious politics that went on. Tafewa Balewa, the prime minister, sometimes rudely, even ruthlessly, shut up some regional premier or federal minister, including my own. The Sardauna and his advisor never said anything. When I later told what had been going on to my former New Zealand permanent secretary and friend, who was entitled to know, he congratulated me and told me that I had won completely. If he had not told me so, I would not have known. Pius was not at this meeting even though his premier was.

The first national plan was adopted with some fanfare in parliament. The plan was published, and I have a beautiful copy signed by my minister and my staff. (I also have a signed deluxe copy of Pius' revised *National Accounts*, without the name of Teddy Jackson, an original coauthor.) The published version of the plan was somewhat reduced in content from its original form. I had worked out the regional distribution of all projects and was rather proud of my work. However, the biggest federal works, including the Niger Dam, or as it had to be called for reasons whose political origins lay in the past long before my time, the Kainji Dam,[16] were in the Northern Region. It turned out that most federal projects were in the North. This was politically unacceptable. The three Northern permanent secretaries – of finance, development and, I believe, agriculture – appeared in my office to protest and demand the excision of this analysis on the grounds that these projects were not truly regional but of national interest. My argument that all projects were presumably of national interest made no impression. I was then a little over 1.80 meters tall; the three Northerners were each a whole head taller than I was. It was a startling performance, with some threatening overtones. I presume that the three acted on orders of the Sardauna. Actually, I had been on good personal terms with each of them, but I also observed that each behaved differently and was more relaxed when he was alone with me than when some other Northern permanent secretary was present. Evidently, each owed his loyalty and power to a different Northern personality, about which I knew nothing.

At the end of my tour of duty, my wife and older son came to Nigeria and we were planning our trip home around the world, tourist class as I had negotiated it with the Ford Foundation on the advice of my Harvard friend, who had originally suggested me for the job. I introduced them, of course, to

---

[16] Kainji Dam was built along the Niger River in 1968 in the area on which Old Bussa Town originally stood.

my minister. Waziri Ibrahim had asked us to come to his office and he had summoned the American ambassador. He then made a speech, telling the ambassador that because of me all Americans would be trusted. Well, perhaps so. The minister had urged me to stay for a second tour of duty but I had steadfastly refused. I pointed out to him that I had done what I could and had brought my assignment to a successful conclusion. I simply did not want to be away from my family for so long a period again. I am sure that if I had acceded to his wishes, he would have been somewhat suspicious that I wanted to make myself indispensable. In any case, Godfrey had warned me that times had changed and that no white man would ever again be in my position, a warning that was quite unnecessary because my own political sense had told me the same thing. The fact remains that I had an experience which perhaps no other white man had before me or will ever have again: to be at the centre of policy making of an independent African country, and not just as an adviser.

One final matter. Normally, when a foreign top advisor or top civil servant left, there was a lousy dinner at the Federal Palace Hotel, to which not everybody invited came. There was a short speech, a present of sorts, perhaps a watch and good-bye. In my case Godfrey Lardner gave a highlife[17] party in his house. My African colleagues from all the regions came, and the only white people present were my family and, I do not quite remember whom else, perhaps also Lyle and Ann Hansen. It was the first time that I knew that I had not only been trusted, but that they actually truly liked me. It is this memory that I treasure to this day.

REFERENCES

Abah, Sonde. 2000. 'The Sardauna of Sokoto'. In *People in TheNEWS 1900–1999. A Survey of Nigerians of the 20th Century*, 153–155. Lagos: Independent Communications Limited.

Adekanmbi, Dotun. 2000. 'The Lone Ranger'. In *People in TheNEWS 1900–1999. A Survey of Nigerians of the 20th Century*, 79–89. Lagos: Independent Communications Limited.

Anonymous. 1975. *Who's Who in the United Nations and Related Agencies*. Detroit, MI: Omnigraphics, Inc.

Anyaegbunam, Ngozi. 1992. *Waziri Ibrahim: Politics without Bitterness*. Lagos: Daily Times of Nigeria.

---

[17] 'Highlife' refers to a form of dance music that was very popular in West Africa at the time.

Blaug, Mark. Ed. 1986. *Who's Who in Economics: A Biographical Dictionary of Major Economists, 1700–1986*. 2nd ed. Cambridge, Mass.: MIT Press.

Clark, Trevor. 1991. *A Right Honourable Gentleman: Abubakar from the Black Rock: A Narrative Chronicle of the Life and Times of Nigeria's Alhaji Sir Abubakar Tafawa 'Balewa*. London: E. Arnold.

Faaland, Just, and Hans-Erik Dahl. 1968a. *The Economy of Kenya. An Econometric Study of Structural Relationships 1956–1965*. Bergen: Chr. Michelsen Institute.

————. 1968b. *The Economy of Tanzania. An Econometric Study of Structural Relationships 1956 to 1965 with Projections of Trade and Resource Gaps for 1970 and 1975*. Bergen: Chr. Michelsen Institute.

————. 1968c. *The Economy of Uganda. An Econometric Study of Structural Relationships 1956 to 1965 with Projections of Trade and Resource Gaps for 1970 and 1975*. Bergen: Chr. Michelsen Institute.

Faaland, Just, and J. R. Parkinson. 1986. *The Political Economy of Development*. New York: St. Martin's Press.

Kirk-Greene, Anthony H. M. 1982. 'Margery Perham and Colonial Administration'. In Frederick Madden and D. K. Fieldhouse, eds., *Oxford and the Idea of Commonwealth: Essays Presented to Sir Edgar Williams*, 122–143. London: Croom Helm.

Mabogunje, Akin L. 2000. 'The Seeker after Truth'. In *People in TheNEWS 1900–1999. A Survey of Nigerians of the 20ᵗʰ Century*, 17–20. Lagos: Independent Communications Limited.

Makinde, Bankole. Ed. 2001. *Newswatch Who's Who in Nigeria*. 2ⁿᵈ edition. Ikeja, Lagos: Newswatch Books Limited.

New School. 2002. 'Nicholas Kaldor (1908–1986)'. http://cepa.newschool.edu/hetprofiles/kaldor.htm [accessed October 23, 2002].

Osso, Nyaknno (ed.). 1990. *Newswatch Who's Who in Nigeria*. Ikeja, Lagos: Newswatch Communications Ltd.

Paden, John N. 1986. *Ahmadu Bello Sardauna of Sokoto: Values and Leadership in Nigeria*. London: Hodder and Stoughton.

Romer-Friedman, Peter. 1998. 'Professor, Economic Adviser Dies at 82'. *The Michigan Daily*, February 23. http://www.umich.edu [accessed September 23, 2002].

Uzoatu, Mazim. 2000. 'The Golden Voice'. In *People in TheNEWS 1900–1999. A Survey of Nigerians of the 20ᵗʰ Century*, 141–142. Lagos: Independent Communications Limited.

3

RETURN TO SCOTT HALL:
A TRIBUTE TO PIUS OKIGBO

Sterling Stuckey

There were no more than thirty or so blacks at Northwestern in my years as an undergraduate. Apart from Pius, I do not recall there having been any in graduate school, though there were probably a few. With no social life available to us beyond what we were able to fashion for ourselves off campus, it was a lonely experience, I suspect, for nearly all of us. Much larger numbers, however, might have reduced my chances of having met Pius because it was something of an event to encounter blacks when there were so few. The absence of a social life for black undergraduates together with the presence of talented and committed teachers provided an ideal climate for focusing on one's academic work. The main means of emotional and spiritual gratification had to be found through books as well, and that is why my friendship with Pius proved to be of such lasting value to me.

Our meetings were almost always by accident. After all, he was much older, a graduate student in a demanding discipline, and I was a mere undergraduate. And yet the world scene was the pressing backdrop to my relationship with him, for we were, in a sense, both colonial subjects, though no such dramatic connection was ever articulated by either of us. I met Pius in The Grill at Scott Hall, Northwestern's principal meeting place of black students at the time. The Grill was a place at which we sometimes ate lunch or dinner, and stopped by to take lighter refreshments and to talk. It was usually late in the day, when it was not very crowded, that Pius and I talked. Despite the fact that he was considerably older than I, I talked to him more often than to anyone else, especially about matters of consequence. He certainly did not distance himself from younger students or from African

Americans. Though the name of Nnamdi Azikiwe never came up, Pius's regard for him probably explains, in some measure, his openness to those of African descent in America, for Azikiwe's interest in Pan-Africanism was well-established in Africa and abroad by the time Pius arrived in America.

Whatever the case, however, Pius conveyed something in our first encounters, beyond the consideration of books, that set me at ease each time I saw him. And yet I do not recall conversations with him that did not begin with or lead to discussions of books. But that is not why I approached him. I approached him because of a much larger issue. Having been an admirer of W. E. B. DuBois in high school, I had for some years been interested in Africa. In fact, Africa was the one great hope of some of my generation and there was nothing about Pius that did not confirm that hope. That being the case, I probably got something of a distorted view of African possibilities for achievement from having focused so concretely on Pius as the example before me, for he was in no sense typical of Africa or, more generally, of human possibility.

He shattered every stereotype I had heard about Africa and people of African descent. Though we probably did not talk more than a dozen times overall, the nature of the talks endeared him to me. Young and somewhat reserved, he was nonetheless as accessible as anyone I have encountered in the academic community. In fact, I doubt that he was ever in Scott Hall alone when I was there that I did not seek him out. When I think of it, and recall how seriously he was preparing himself for what he was to become, I marvel that he was so generous with his time.

In my last brief meetings with him, before his departure for Oxford, there was some discussion about my possibly buying his car before he left, but I could not afford it. After he left for England in 1954, I did not see him again. The Pius that I met at Northwestern – the young Pius – is mainly the Pius that I have known. He was among the first wave of African students to come to America following World War II and I was one of the first African American students, through him, to be a part of that process.

Though I did not know how he had come to study at Northwestern, there was no mistaking that he was brilliant, at home in numerous disciplines beyond economics. Indeed, his intellect was exceptionally striking and wide-ranging, and he seemed as natural a scholar as I had known. But he, too, was only human. Preparing for a period of exams with unflagging intensity, he once remarked to me that he was losing some of his hair. He was confident enough to admit that he had been under great stress without exactly saying so. I then resolved that if ever, owing to hard work, I lost some of my hair it would be all right because Pius had once lost some of his. I, of course, was to lose mine in a quite different way, as you can see. After the lapse of decades without having thought of what he told me about *his* hair, I now take it as a compliment that he shared such information, for it was, in fact, the only thing really private that I recall him sharing with me. He once said that he was well prepared to study at Northwestern and at Oxford, but that was, by then, public knowledge.

From an African American perspective, the racial horizon seemed dominated by storm clouds in the late forties and fifties, and as sensitive blacks reflected on the condition of the black American, a degree of psychic and spiritual pain seemed inescapable. In truth, a certain self-loathing, building since the close of World War II, had found a relatively secure place in the upper reaches of black leadership. It was a period in which mainstream black leadership did not encourage pride in one's blackness, to say nothing of seriously affirming one's African ancestry. Indeed, interest in integration had reached such a stage that the leader of the most distinguished civil rights organization, the NAACP, recommended bleach cream as a possible solution to the race problem in America. With such a failure of leadership, it is small wonder that an occasional Northwestern black student would not speak to other blacks, small as their numbers were, when encountering them on campus. Too small to be a significant force, such students seemed to be saying, yet because of that we could not afford, most of us felt, to reduce our numbers still further by ignoring each other.

Some of us at Northwestern, and at other schools, looked to Africa with increasing hope, for it was thought that independence for black Africa would favour black liberation in the Americas. At the time, I was not aware that Pius had been chosen to play a leadership role in an independent Nigeria. A lot that was unspoken would have been taken up had I known. Had I known, conversation, at my urging would have turned to politics in African and to Pan-African concerns, for the atmosphere was not altogether inimical to interest in such matters by younger African Americans.

In the early fifties there was talk of Jomo Kenyatta and the crisis in Kenya, and signs at Elevated stops on the South Side of Chicago were scrawled with the slogan: 'Free Kenyatta!' A bearded white man made the same call while passing out leaflets beneath the Elevated tracks. He seemed radical in appearance and I was struck even then by what appeared, at least for the Chicago area, to have been the loneliness of his crusade. But as an undergraduate, I was not aware of the Council on African Affairs, headed by Paul Robeson and W.E.B. DuBois, nor was I aware of the tiny handful of additional organizations, including The American Society on African Culture (AMSAC), with an interest in Africa. The atmosphere of the Cold War was not conducive to such developments being a part of one's consciousness, nor was one's being a student at a time when loyalty oaths were in vogue.

Having lost contact with Pius, since becoming aware of his death, I have felt the need to return to books he discussed, and to some he recommended. As a consequence of this, I have discovered that I am closer to his spirit and understand, better than ever, his shaping influences in my intellectual development at an impressionable stage of my life. That I did not encounter him in class as a teaching assistant no doubt fostered a more genuine relationship with him, and makes it easier for me now, without any professional barrier between us, to know the character of the man. What was clear at the start, however, is that reading the authors he admired was such a source of joy that I read them, never thinking of the time and energy invested in the journey.

I am not certain how Pius came to recommend that I read certain books. Perhaps, after having talked to me, he decided that there were particular books I would benefit from reading. What is more likely is that I pursued references made by him in the course of conversation, and asked him about additional books to read, placing the books about which he seemed most excited on my reading list beside the books assigned for classes by my professors. It was the most exciting period of my life as an undergraduate, for I was also, in English B10, reading John Milton *(Samson Agonistes)*, Jonathon Swift *(Gulliver's Travels)* and the Greek playwrights, among other authors. The books suggested by Pius were no less a part of my education, enabling me to range widely among brilliant authors who wanted to transform the contemporary world. Though I do not recall a single conversation with him about colonialism in the world or about racism in America, the books he suggested that I read were very much related to such concerns.

I began with a favourite of his, Harold Laski's *Faith, Reason and Civilization*, which affected me greatly, then went on to Laski's *The American Democracy, Liberty and the Modern State and The Holmes/Laski Correspondence*. Not only were Laski's references, especially in *Faith, Reason and Civilization*, dazzling in reach but his special way of phrasing as he moved from one thought to another in building an argument was of interest. Laski on Henry James and T.S. Eliot is inspiring in *Faith, Reason and Civilization*. He writes:

> Henry James may not have understood that the morals of a society in which a small class of wealthy people are so parasitic upon the labour of the masses that they are predestined to corruption; but at least he recognized the corruption when he encountered it... Mr. Eliot saw that same corruption; yet it did not occur to him ...that a church which does

not insist upon the inclusion of the masses within the culture of a civilization is bound to fail, in the long run, to perform that task of moral elevation he has assigned to it...The truth is... that a small, wealthy class had made the morals of our civilization no more than an argument for the defense of its own claims (Laski 1944, 196).

Laski's belief that service to others is the secret to self-respect, that there is no real answer to the fundamental problem of service 'save in our power to recreate the climate of hope and eagerness among ordinary people' was a formulation that Pius was never to lose sight of. Moreover, Laski's reference to those men and women who built 'a temple of refuge for the human spirit where there can be preserved that right to dream', which 'is the source of [the] power to win mastery over the hostile forces of the universe', must have resonated deeply with Pius (Laski 1944, 81). A favourite of students from the colonized world and an intellectual with an interest in black Americans, Laski's scholarship, especially *Faith, Reason and Civilization*, provided an exciting beginning. Some years later, after Pius and I were no longer at Northwestern, when there was controversy over certain features of the Holmes-Laski correspondence, I wondered what Pius thought of the matter, hoping one day to discuss it with him.

Pius directed me to Simone de Beauvoir. I recognized immediately that it was simply not possible, in Cold War America or immediately after World War II, to have experienced the sort of intellectual excitement, except vicariously, that is found in *The Mandarins*. But the hope in the Soviet experiment expressed by Laski was, I could not fail to notice, seriously questioned by characters in *The Mandarins*, and there were intimations of the moral collapse of communism that was to come. Having read *The Mandarins*, I moved on to *America Day to Day* and later to *The Second Sex*. Contending positions and various options came increasingly into focus as I read the books that were important to Pius. But the sympathy of the authors to socialism was unmistakable.

Because of Pius, I came to know Nehru's *Toward Freedom: The Autobiography of Jawaharlal Nehru*, *Glimpses of World History* and *The Discovery of India*. Since Pius was especially interested in the Indian model of economic advancement, it is not surprising that he studied Nehru's writings and mentioned him in conversation. I did not hesitate, therefore, to read Nehru and found his prose, for clarity and elegance of expression, utterly devoid of pretension. But it was more than his lucid and beautifully measured language that won my admiration; his anticolonialism, his erudition and his refinement of spirit were everywhere evident. Nehru, of course, wrote *Glimpses of World History*, his letters to Indira, while imprisoned for struggling for the independence of India. In *Glimpses* Nehru wrote: 'Religion, science, the love of one's own country, all were prostituted to one end – the exploitation of the weaker and industrially more backward peoples of the earth'. Surely he spoke for large numbers of anticolonial subjects in writing, in one of his last letters to Indira: 'All of us...are looking forward expectantly to the future as it unrolls itself and becomes the present. Some await the outcome with hope, others with fear'. A call to action followed:

> It is easy to admire the beauties of the universe and to live in a world of thought and imagination. But to try and escape in this way from the unhappiness of others, caring little what happens to them, is no sign of courage or fellow-feeling... People avoid action often because they are afraid of the consequences, for action means risk and danger. Danger seems terrible from a distance; it is not so bad if you have a close look at it. And often it is a pleasant companion, adding to the zest and delight of life... All of us have our choice of living in the valleys below, with their unhealthy mists and fogs, but giving a measure of bodily security; or of climbing the high mountains, with risk and danger for companions, to breathe the pure air above and take joy in the distant views, and welcome the rising sun (Nehru 1962b, 84, 288, 294).

The writers Pius appears to have admired most wanted to see the dawn of that new day to which Nehru referred.

While reading LaRay Denzer's (2001, 4) 'In Memoriam' tribute in *News and Events*, my eyes went immediately to the photo of Pius and professors Jane Guyer, Jean Herskovits and Ikem Okoye. He looked very much the same as when I last saw him in 1954, except for the white hair. The fact that I had not seen him since that time heightened the sadness that I felt, and I considered certain missed opportunities – not having been present when he appeared at the fiftieth anniversary celebration of the founding of the African Studies Program; not having met his daughter when she was an undergraduate at Northwestern, and above all not having made my way to Nigeria at some point to renew our friendship. Not knowing of his closeness to Frances Herskovits, with whom I had lunch on several occasions in the sixties, I reflected that had I known the two knew each other I could surely, when with her, have begun to discover things about him I would not have known until recently – such as, for example, that he was close to Azikiwe. Since I have found numerous admiring letters from Azikiwe to Paul Robeson in the Robeson manuscript collection, had Pius and I talked about Azikiwe or Robeson, I almost certainly would have discovered a rewarding line of inquiry into Pan-Africanism. And some discussion of DuBois would have followed.

Pius left for Oxford in 1954, a year before I graduated from Northwestern. But he had put me on the important trail of books to which I returned on hearing of his death and that has rekindled the spirit of our relationship as nothing else could for me. I am rather proud of myself that nearly fifty years ago, as young as I was, I chose him as my guide to learning.

Last night I paid a return visit to Scott Hall, which is now for me hallowed ground.

REFERENCES

Denzer, LaRay. 2001. 'In Memoriam'. *Program of African Studies News and Events* 11(2):4.

Laski, Harold J. 1944. *Faith Reason and Civilisation: An Essay in Historical Analysis.* London: Victor Gollancz Ltd.

Nehru, Jawaharlal. 1962a [1942]. *Glimpses of World History: Being Further Letters to His Daughter, Written in Prison, and Containing a Rambling Account of History for Young People.* 2nd Indian edition. Bombay and New York: Asia Publishing House.

Nehru, Jawaharlal [edited by Saul Kussiel Padover]. 1962b. *Nehru on World History.* Bloomington, Indiana University Press.

PART II: OKIGBO AND THE EVOLUTION OF THE NIGERIAN STATE

EMT D. OJUKWO AND THE EVOLUTION OF
THE NIGERIAN STATE

4

LOVE'S LABOUR LOST? OKIGBO AND THE TRAVAILS OF FISCAL FEDERALISM

Adigun Agbaje

Money is the root of all evil.
– Popular Nigerian proverb

My argument is that we must begin now to re-arrange the architecture of our policies and actions to face squarely the new challenges of the 21st Century... Our task now is to secure that future.
– Okigbo (1993a, 280).

INTRODUCTION

In the period since May 29, 1999, following the inauguration of the Fourth Republic, resource control has emerged as the defining element of Nigeria's putative federal system. Before now, such other concepts as quota system, federal character, derivation, power sharing and power shift have taken their turn in the limelight as lightning rods of aspects of the stresses and strains of Nigerian federalism in relation to matters arising from the management of individual and group access to public resources, and continue still to compound and reinforce the distributive tendencies in the theory and practice of that federal system (Suberu 1999, Suberu and Agbaje 1998). The distributive logic of Nigeria's brand of federalism as expressed in various forms over the years explains the salience of fiscal issues and fiscal federalism in the polity. Essentially, fiscal issues cover matters of public finance as they relate to the treasury of the state and its revenue and expenditure. Such issues tend to be even more complex in highly divided societies operating federal systems, which give constitutional recognition to more than one tier of government, since they involve a complex set of structures and relationships.

Despite the tone of recent public discourse, which suggests the contrary, fiscal federalism is not a new issue in Nigeria's political history. As is clear below, as far back as 1965, Okigbo's *Nigerian Public Finance* addressed the evolution, structure, dynamics and controversies in Nigeria's fiscal system from the beginning of the colonial era to the First Republic in the 1960s. It is also easy to forget, in the context of the cacophony of contemporary voices, that as far back as the early 1950s, the leaders of Western Nigeria threatened to secede over the control of the resources in Lagos while those of Northern Nigeria issued similar threats with reference to the control of the emerging national parliament (Ayoade 1973, 1998; Tamuno 1970, 1998).

Stresses arising from fiscal federalism are not a uniquely Nigerian problem. As Tamuno (1998, 14) has aptly put it, 'Nigeria's example gives credence to the general (though not absolute) rule that emphasis on economics constituted the 'first concern' of a federalist or quasi-federalist arrangement'. It is also becoming increasingly clear at the global level that 'the functions and financing of local and regional government are major issues in the evolution of economic policy and in broad social and political developments'. Thus, 'reform of the fiscal relations between central and subnational governments is an urgent priority in many countries', thanks in part to new patterns of interaction, integration and disintegration within and among countries in the context of globalization that have created 'a new market environment within which fiscal relations are established among countries and among regions within countries'. The reality now is that:

> In every major region of the world, the assignment of fiscal responsibilities and resources among different levels of government, the coordination of fiscal policies among governments at the same or different levels, and a host of related political and social issues are matters of intense interest to policy makers' (Wildasin 1997, 2–3).

In the light of Pius Okigbo's works, this chapter examines Nigeria's experience with fiscal federalism. The central argument here is that while that experience resembles several other experiences such as, for instance, the tendency for fiscal concentration in central government to increase with the age of federations, the Nigerian experience has its own peculiar dimensions. The specificities of the Nigerian experience derive from its political history and political economy, ultimately revolving around the country's lack of meaningful experience and skills in the management of the federal arrangement in a democratic environment. It is for this reason that the distributive nature of Nigeria's putative federalism tends to emphasize separatist tendencies instead of initiating and facilitating moves towards cooperation, promotes consociational power sharing over and above integrative power sharing, and increasingly entrenches identity politics instead of interest politics, thereby promoting differences in the body politic while understating similarities.

OKIGBO'S LEGACY

As indicated above, one of the earlier detailed accounts of fiscal issues is offered in Okigbo's *Nigerian Public Finance* (1965a). This book was initiated in 1962 while Dr Okigbo was serving, at the request of the government of the United Kingdom, as a member of a fiscal commission to provide for the devolution of fiscal authority from Kenya's central government to regions that were then about to be created. In that book, it is argued that Nigeria's fiscal system up to 1962 had been influenced by the constitutional changes Nigeria experienced under British colonial rule up to Independence in 1960. The work places Nigeria's fiscal system in proper historical perspective, detailing the interplay of structure and processes in determining the evolving fiscal relations among the tiers of government as well as the role of the public sector in the development of the country. It offers rare insights into the early phases of Nigeria's fiscal structure and relationships, the development of direct taxation, the finance of local and regional authorities, revenues of the central government and prospects for the future.

Over the years, Okigbo's works continued to provide rare and rich insights into fiscal issues in Nigeria, reflecting and often seeking to temper the moods of the moment. For instance, he did pioneering work on Nigeria's national accounts (1960, 1962), saving and investment through government budgeting (1965), Nigeria's financial system (1981), national development planning (1989), oil and national planning (1983) and the philosophy of the development process (in a three-volume work published in 1987 and 1993). The last-mentioned trilogy of essays considered various aspects of the structure and history of the Nigerian economy, obstacles to planning fiscal policies, a historical survey of revenue allocation in Nigeria and a critique of the report of the 1977 Aboyade technical committee on revenue allocation. Between 1979 and 1980, Okigbo chaired a presidential commission on revenue allocation. He regularly issued comments on specific national budgets and advocated planning the Nigerian economy for less dependence on oil.

As is clear below, what Okigbo offers in all this is a perspective on fiscal federalism that goes beyond the tendency of Nigerians to reduce this issue to one of vertical revenue allocation among the levels of government even as he includes this in his own considerations. For instance, in *Nigerian*

Public Finance (1965a), he details the extent to which the regions up to the early 1960s were fiscally independent of the central government in law and in practice, and complements this with a rich consideration of horizontal fiscal relations and statistics among the regional governments themselves. Beyond such issues, however, Okigbo devoted even more energy to wider issues relating to overspecialization in the area of revenue sources, economics and political uncertainties as well as the wider contexts of the development process as these impinged on fiscal matters.

By the 1970s, Nigeria had moved from overdependence or, in the words of Okigbo, overspecialization on export crops to petroleum as the main source of government revenue. This, for Okigbo, was a trend to be watched. He declared that:

> Most African or, indeed, Third World countries depend for their revenues each on a single commodity... They are, as it were, paying the penalty for what can best be described as premature overspecialization.... Nigeria faces the risk not only of progressive erosion of the price of petroleum but of technological developments in energy sources and use... (Okigbo 1993b, 121).

This overspecialization creates problems for fiscal management, for it literally creates in perpetuity an expectation of vulnerability, even if the commodity has changed from export crops to oil over time. As another economist has observed, following the collapse of oil prices in the world market during the Second Republic, 'there was a nation-wide replay in the late 1970s of the vicissitudes of government finance that characterized the late 1950s when Nigeria's export crops (particularly cocoa) tumbled in the world market' (Philips 1981, 17–18). Such vulnerability was subsequently demonstrated in the early 1980s as well as in the 1990s.

For this reason, economic and political uncertainties, instability and risks occupy a pride of place in Okigbo's analyses of Nigeria's fiscal situation. He observed:

> At the national level, we often find that what looks like an innocuous act by the rulers of a country may spark off from the public reactions that may be wilder than could have been anticipated. Or, they may unsuspectingly bring in rules or take actions that affect adversely the interest of some members of the international community that may react to protect their interest (Okigbo 1993b, 113–114).

At the local level, the movement from overdependence on export crops to the overdependence on oil as the public revenue source has had consequences for the polity. The general point is that the political configuration of the elite and the masses around the geography of resource exploitation for public revenue determines to a large extent the nature of risks, uncertainty and instability that this can engender as well as the policy options open to government. As Okigbo and others have shown, to the extent that the major sources of public revenue up to the 1960s were the regions dominated by major ethnic groups, sections of which also controlled the central government, the principle of derivation held sway in revenue sharing among the centre and the regions – ensuring that areas providing revenue benefited more in its sharing. However, to the extent that the major sources of public revenue after the 1970s were oil-bearing communities peopled largely by ethnic minorities, the principle of derivation was held in abeyance or at best de-emphasized for about two decades until the oil communities exploded in frustrated rage.

Before returning to its implications for the derivation issue, it is appropriate to highlight the other elements of Okigbo's analyses of the dangers of overspecialization and its risks, and more broadly with uncertainty and instability. These include the dangers due to technological developments (especially in regard of the race for synthetic substitutes for iron, steel, oil and copper, among others), foreign exchange fluctuations and political and policy instability. Concerning some of these issues, Okigbo concluded:

> There are...very many factors that may influence the value of the domestic currency in relation to the foreign currency. One of these is clearly the extent to which there is stability in financial, fiscal or monetary policies. If there is clearly a strong indication of fiscal or monetary indiscipline, any one intending to make forward contracts involving foreign currency obligations will tend to hedge by not committing his resources to long-term investment... Consequently, expenditures extending beyond the shortest term will be deferred as a form of hedging (Okigbo 1993b, 122–123).

On the specific issue of political risk and the long-drawn political transition of the late 1980s and early 1990s, he observed that:

> In the face of...strong political instability, economic as well as political policies face strong uncertainties. Whilst business can cope, to some degree, with political instability reflected in frequent changes of governments, it is difficult to conduct meaningful business in an atmosphere of strong instability of policies... In Nigeria, there is the doubt being raised in the minds of investors, Nigerian and foreign, as to

how much business can and will survive the process of re-democratization. Will the policies pursued these past...years still be in place when democratically elected governments take over or will the democratic push lead to the replacement of the main planks of these policies? These questions must agitate our minds for they lie at the core of the continued growth of our economies and the well being of the bulk of our peoples (Okigbo 1993b, 123, 125).

THE TRAVAILS OF FISCAL FEDERALISM

In considerations of the travails of Nigeria's fiscal federalism, relatively more attention has been paid to horizontal and vertical revenue allocation/sharing within and among the levels of government. Less attention has been paid to such issues as the matching of resources with responsibilities, tax powers, diversification of revenue sources, budgeting in the context of separation of powers and the general level of institutional capacity for monitoring and control, public debt management, as well as efficiency issues in sectoral and economic management as these relate to government expenditure, among others. In the period between 1914 and now, the pendulum of fiscal powers has swung from centralization to decentralization and back to centralization. While the two protectorates of North and South continued to be governed separately by the colonial regime after the 1914 amalgamation, between 1926–1927 and 1947–1948 fiscal years, the fiscal powers of the protectorates were unified with their revenue and expenditure accounts centralized and brought together under one head (see Tobi 1989; Adedeji 1969). After 1946, some fiscal responsibility devolved on the newly created three regions, along with a measure of administrative autonomy. The regions, however, had no legal powers to appropriate revenue for regional expenditure, giving the central government 'a high degree of fiscal supremacy as the regions had no autonomy except to prepare their own budgets and could only execute them subject to approval by the centre' (Tobi 1989, 142).

In terms of government expenditure, this period has been characterized by Phillips (1981, 9–17) as one that witnessed the emergence of the Service State, in contrast to the 1950s that was presided over by what he calls the Incipient Paternal State, the 1960s that witnessed the emergence of the Dislocated Paternal State and the rise thereafter of the Paternal State. He contends that:

> ...it is possible...to attempt to define a Service State as one in which the scope of government activity is kept to the minimum required to enable economy and society to function, principally under private initiative... A Paternal State on the other hand...attempts to cater di-

rectly for most of the needs of the citizens and regulates and controls their social and economic activities rather much more comprehensively (p.9).

Up to the 1940s, therefore, the colonial state emphasized minimum government. The focus in public finance was on recurrent expenditure over and above capital and/or development activities, with a tendency to ensure budget surpluses (Phillips 1981, 10). The 1951 constitution gave more substantive autonomy to the regions by adopting a semi-federal system of government along with a Westminster-type parliament elevated from a consultative to a legislative body. The regional councils' powers to legislate, however, were subject to the approval of the regional governor, and they had very little power over tax. The power to set, collect and distribute revenues from tax remained with the central government. Although the 1954 constitution signalled the formal adoption of federalism in Nigeria, it continued to locate important tax powers in the centre.

Against this background, Nigerian politicians now in control of the legislature and executive in the regions mounted pressures to ensure that control of local resources shifted to the regions to provide the means with which to execute their programs. Subsequently, a decision was taken at the 1953 constitutional conference to regionalize the marketing boards system for export crops, then the mainstay of the economy. Regional governments also received the powers to tax personal incomes while regional governments subsequently attained parity with the central government in the area of revenue allocation (the regions getting 50.4 percent to the central government's 49.6 percent in the 1959/60 fiscal year).

The coups of 1966, the onset of military rule and the 1967–1970 civil war reversed this trend. In this context, 'the federal government...gained legitimate opportunities to appropriate the lion's share of total resources ostensibly to prosecute the war and reconstruct the postcivil war economy' (Tobi 1989, 143). The unitary structure of military rule, rising oil revenue and the exigencies of the war turned the new federal system into a de facto unitary arrangement and 'permitted a very rapid and large expansion of the level and scope of government activity without significant increases in the burden of tax revenue on the citizens' (Phillips 1981, 17). While this burden of oil revenue was perceived largely as being borne by the external market, in the long run, it turned out to be a burden borne disproportionately by the oil-bearing communities. Government's inadequate attention to the local dimension of the burden explains the restiveness and anger that became the hallmark of oil-bearing communities' interaction with oil companies and the various levels of government after the 1990s.

Highlights of the period from 1960 to the late 1980s include a phenomenal increase in government expenditure: the federal government accounted for the greater share – up from about one billion naira in 1970–1971 to almost 12 billion in 1980. Not only did the federal government dominate the fiscal system, but it also controlled the oil industry, which accounted for between 80 percent to over 90 percent of government revenue (see Phillips 1981, 17; Obi 1998; Ekpo 1994; Olowononi 1998; Mbanefoh and Egwaikhide 1998; Adesina 1998; Aliyu 1977, 134–135; Phillips 1971, 1976, 1980; Dudley 1966). From the late 1960s, the federal military government gradually took over or subsidized the functions of state governments while positioning itself not only to control the revenue allocation system but also to direct a disproportionately large share of the country's resources to itself. According to Suberu (1999, 93), 'this centralized redistribution of economic resources has been achieved by the elaboration of specific vertical and horizontal rules for intergovernmental revenue-sharing' such as:

1. The collection or administration by the Federal Government of the most lucrative financial resources and tax revenues, including the petroleum profits tax, mining rents and royalties, company income tax and export and import duties.

2. The allocation to the Federal Government of federally collected revenues exceeding the combined shares of the state and local authorities.

3. The direct administration by the Federal Government of all funds set aside under the national revenue-sharing scheme for special purposes or programs, including the amelioration of national ecological problems, the development of the new federal capital territory and the rehabilitation of mineral-producing areas.

4. The progressive institutionalization of direct financial relationships between the federal and local governments and of the rights of the localities to participate directly in the national revenue-sharing scheme.

5. The progressive reduction in the proportions of federal statutory financial allocations to the states simultaneously with an expansion of the local authorities' shares of these allocations.

In addition, the progressive splitting of the federating units into more states and local governments after the 1960s – to the extent that the country now has 36 states and 774 local government areas – in the short-term boosted decentralization of government expenditure but in the long run has led to a concentration process tilting 'the pattern of inter-tier expenditure towards the Federal/Central government' (Phillips 1981, 19), with more government functions being concentrated in the hands of the latter (see also Mbanefoh and Egwaikhide 1998, 219–220; Mbanefoh 1986). The Federal Government's decision, in the face of economic and infrastructural crises from the 1980s, to establish and manage special accounts (including the Stabilization Fund, Dedicated Accounts, Petroleum Trust Fund and Education Tax Fund), further accelerated this process. Much of the funds paid into these accounts should have been paid into the federation account for sharing among the three tiers of government (federal, state and local).

A major development in the evolution of guiding principles for revenue allocation in Nigeria in the postcivil war era ensued from the reports of the Aboyade and Okigbo Commissions (see Federal Republic of Nigeria 1979, 1980). Together, these two commissions not only de-emphasized the principle of derivation (Olowononi 1998, 250) established by the Phillipson fiscal commission of 1942 but also argued for a greater share of revenue for the federal government (Phillipson 1948). This shift to the centre was dramatically noticeable in an earlier commission's work. In the context of the divisiveness that preceded the outbreak of the civil war as well as the creation of new states in 1967, the federal military government, in the middle of the war in 1968, set up an Interim Revenue Allocation Review Committee (IRARC) with Chief I. O. Dina as chair. The committee, now known as the Dina Commission, was persuaded by the view that 'fiscal arrangements in this country should reflect the new spirit of unity to which the nation is dedicated'. It went on to state 'it is in the spirit of this new-found unity that we have viewed all the sources of revenue of this country as the common funds of the country to be used for executing the kinds of programs that can maintain this unity' (quoted in Adesina 1998, 236).

This concern for unity and the fiscal strengthening of the centre provided the background to the ostensibly less political and more technical reports of the Aboyade and Okigbo Commissions in the postwar period. The Aboyade group recommended that the federation account be distributed as follows: 57 percent to the central government, 30 percent to state governments and 10 percent to local governments. Recommendations of the Okigbo Commission, as endorsed by the Revenue Allocation Act for 1981, provided for 55 percent for the central government, 30.5 percent for state governments, 10 percent for local governments and 4.5 percent for special funds. They also provided for federal control of these special funds and included the Federal Capital Authority as a unit separate from the central government in the vertical sharing scheme. On this issue, apparent shifts in Okigbo's position have to be contextualized. His commission actually submitted one majority report and two minority reports on aspects of their mandate (Adesina 1998, 237). Even as the commission reflected mainstream centrist sentiments in the decade after the war, Okigbo's less centrist position during the war as well as his view in the 1990s that 55 percent of the federation account should go to derivation, reflect changes in the political ecology as well as his location as Igbo, democrat, devolutionist and nationalist in Nigeria's political geography.

The adoption of the recommendations of the Okigbo commission led to a landmark decision of the Supreme Court that nullified the ensuing Revenue Allocation Act of 1981 following a suit brought against the act by the (then) Bendel State Government, whose jurisdiction covered some of the most productive and expansive oil producing areas in the country (including the current Edo and Delta states). It had gone to court for a ruling on increased federal share of the federation account and decreasing emphasis on derivation principle in the sharing of the account.

One major gain in the evolving democratic experiment of the Fourth Republic (1999–present) is the opportunity offered for anticentralist forces to challenge the existing order. The Second Republic (1979–1983) allocated only 2 percent of the federation account to the mineral-producing states on the basis of derivation and 1.5 percent for the developmental and ecological needs of such areas. The succeeding Buhari regime (1984–1985) retained these percentages but redefined them as referring only to federally-collected mineral revenues. On its part, the Babangida regime (1985–1993) reduced the percentage of federally-collected mineral revenues accruing to mineral-bearing areas on the basis of derivation from 2 percent to 1 percent while increasing the percentage allocated to such areas for developmental and ecological needs from 1.5 percent to 3 percent. In the Fourth Republic, however, not less than 13 percent of the revenue accruing to the federation account from any natural resources will be allocated to the area from which such resources are extracted (as provided for by section 162(2) of the 1999 constitution). Section 162(1) abolishes all special accounts apart from the federation account into which all revenues collected by the government of the federation, except the proceeds from certain personal income taxes (of the armed forces, the police, staff of the foreign ministry and residents of the Federal Capital Territory, Abuja), would be paid.

The opening up of the political process has witnessed agitation, especially by oil-producing states of the South-South geopolitical zone, but also including North Central states with hydroelectric facilities, for a greater share of the benefits of the resources located in their areas. Such agitations have led to counter-agitations. On both sides are extreme and not-so-extreme positions.

On the side of those favouring resource-rich areas, which also tend to be peopled by political and ethnic minorities, are those calling for total control of their resources. For these activists, such resource-rich areas should only pay tax on their resources to the federation as and when exploited. Therefore, they advocate either resource control or something close to secession. Less maximalist is the view within this group that what is required is for derivation to account for a higher percentage of allocations from the federation account (e.g., Sagay 2001a, 2001b, 2001c; Babalola 2001; Adisa 2001; Onimode 2001; Anonymous 2000, 2001; Fiakpa 1998). Often, these demands are couched in a request for 'true' or 'real' federalism (Daisi 1998; Adedeji 2001; Adeyemo and Mumuni 2000, 17). As Daisi (1998) argues:

...there is the need for redistributional equity in the appropriation of the nation's resources...the fiscal federalism principle dictates that the revenue allocation formula should be related to the magnitude of fiscal responsibility of each tier of government. A significant element of fiscal federalism is the high degree of fiscal autonomy and decentralization. The principles of derivation and need are principal considerations in the appropriation of financial resources under this model. This principle will help to enhance the stability of the polity and also facilitate the country's efforts at promoting economic prosperity. Such an arrangement also has the added advantage of dousing the extreme acrimony that now characterizes the struggle for political power at the centre... [T]he current excessive concentration of financial resources at the federal level of government (and invariably in the hands of a few people) has been a major constraining factor in the economic liberation of the country.

On the other side of the divide are those who warn that they can carry their opposition to resource control to the battle field; that resource control is a recipe for chaos, especially if every community is to subscribe to the logic of the oil-bearing areas and seek control of its own resources (including food crops and hydroelectric facilities (Anonymous 2001, 1-2, 6; *Tell*, February 21, 1999; Salami 2001; Aderibigbe 2001).

Differences over this issue of resource control are often perceived along the old geopolitical divides of North and South, especially since the platform of the Southern governors' pro-resource control position stands in sharp contrast to the northern Governors' collective opposition to the idea.

Moreover, an attempt to introduce a bill by a South-South member on the issue on the floor of the House of Representatives in May 2001 was rebuffed in a manner that broadly pitched Northern members against their Southern counterparts. The issue, however, is much more complex. For instance, individual Northern governors have publicly expressed support for resource control while at least one governor from the South has sided with the federal government in a suit initiated by the latter seeking the Supreme Court's interpretation of the extent of the federating units' control of resources located in Nigeria's territorial waters.

It is also not a settled matter as to which unit would or should benefit from resource control – should it be the state, in which the resource in question is located, or the communities, or even individuals, in the resource-producing areas? This has pitched oil-bearing communities in Ondo State against their governor, who at one time was accused of using revenues allocated to the state under derivation to develop a new state university located in his village, which, incidentally, is not in the oil-producing area of the state. In such other states as Delta, the youth of the oil-producing communities have engaged their kings and elders in a running battle, while such oil-producing communities have taken on non-oil-producing communities and the state government over the same issue (Bamgbetan 2000).

In the midst of all this, one development that has not attracted the attention it deserves is the decreasing capacity of government in the area of tax collection, a phenomenon occurring simultaneously with the increasing tendency to evade tax by individuals and corporate bodies. The background to this is, of course, the widely acknowledged failure of the Nigerian state to fulfil even the most basic obligations to its citizens such as security, water, electricity, health and basic education (cf. Ipaye 2000; Joseph, Taylor and Agbaje 1996, 300–301).

Yet another issue concerns how to ensure accountability and transparency (see Odion et al. 2001) in fiscal matters. Several governors, ministers and many local government executives are reportedly under investigation by the new anticorruption commission (Oladeji and Olatunji 2001). Allocations to all levels of government have increased significantly, but the popular perception is that these have not translated into a better quality of life for the people. The result is an unabating crisis of confidence in the polity and rising popular frustrations over the inability of the new regime to demonstrate that it is different from the plundering, insensitive, inefficient regime of military rule in the recent and not-so-recent past.

CONCLUSION
The late Pius Okigbo devoted much of his life to inquiring into and disseminating the requirements of fiscal federalism supportive of a good life

for the Nigerian people as well as an efficient and accountable platform for their governments – from the local to the national. In order for the labour of this hero, and those of others past and present, not to have been in vain, Nigerians and those who govern over them require time to learn, by day-to-day failure and successes, how to operate a federal democratic system. A vital requirement is a political and economic culture founded on restraint, social trust and the required skills for bargaining, and devoid of undue haste, impatience and significant disagreement over the fundamentals and ideals of the evolving regime. Since Okigbo's work on fiscal federalism developed over a long career and almost the entire period of Nigerian independence, his arguments and reflections in response to the changing situation can be a major resource in the formation of such a political and economic culture.

REFERENCES

Adedeji, A. 1969. *Nigerian Federal Finance*. London: Hutchinson.

Adedeji, A. 2001. 'The Imperative of Restituting True Federalism'. *Nigerian Tribune* (Ibadan), April 13:21, 28.

Aderibigbe, Y. 2001. 'Resource Control: Looking Beyond the Lure of Crude Oil'. *The Guardian* (Lagos), April 30:8–9.

Adesina, O.C. 1998. 'Revenue Allocation Commissions and the Contradictions in Nigeria's Federalism'. In K. Amuwo, A. Agbaje, R. Suberu and G. Herault, eds., *Federalism and Political Restructuring in Nigeria*, 232–246. Ibadan: Spectrum and Institut français de recherche en Afrique (IFRA).

Adeyemo, W. and M. Mumuni. 2000. 'We Need a Genuine Federation Now! – Akinjide'. *Tell*, February 21:17.

Adisa, T. 2001. 'Panacea for True Federalism'. *Punch* (Lagos), April 16:21.

Aliyu, A.T. 1977. 'The New Revenue Allocation Formula: A Critique'. *Nigerian Journal of Public Affairs* 7:124–137.

Anonymous. 2000. 'South-South Empowerment Front (SSEF) Sues Federal Government on Derivation'. *Guardian* (Lagos), September 21:23, 25.

Anonymous. 2001. 'Governors Insist on New Revenue Formula'. *Punch* (Lagos), January 26:1–2, 6.

Ayoade, J.A.A. 1973. 'Secession Threat as a Redressive Mechanism in Nigerian Federalism'. *Publius: Journal of Federalism* 3(1):57–74.

————. 1998. 'The Federal Character Principle and the Search for National Integration'. In K. Amuwo, A. Agbaje, R. Suberu and G. Herault, eds., *Federalism and Political Restructuring in Nigeria*, 101–120. Ibadan: Spectrum and IFRA.

Babalola, A. 2001. 'Derivation and Statutory Allocation: Matters Arising III'. *Nigerian Tribune* (Ibadan), April 16:7.

Bamgbetan, K. 2000. 'Derivation Crisis in Delta'. *The Punch* (Lagos), September 18:18.

Daisi, K. 1998. 'Towards a Truly Federal Revenue Allocation System'. *Business Times* (Lagos), October 19:5.

Dudley, B. 1966. 'Federalism and the Balance of Political Power in Nigeria'. *Journal of Commonwealth Political Studies*, 4(1):16–29.

Ekpo, Akpan H. 1994. 'Fiscal Federalism: Nigeria's Post-Independence Experience, 1960–90'. *World Development* 22(8):1129–1146.

Federal Republic of Nigeria. 1979. *Report of the Technical Committee on Revenue Allocation under the Military.* Lagos: Federal Government Press.

———— 1980. *Report of the Presidential Commission on Revenue Allocation.* Vols. I–IV. Lagos: Federal Government Press.

Fiakpa, L. 1998. 'Ijaws Gun for Secession'. *Tell* (Lagos), October 26:20–21.

Ipaye, A. 2000. 'Untapped Potential of Withholding Taxes'. *Guardian* (Lagos), September 27:35–36.

Joseph, R.A.S. Taylor and A. Agbaje. 1996. 'Nigeria'. In W. A. Joseph, M. Kesselman and J. Krieger, eds., *Third World Politics at the Crossroads*, 269–345. Lexington, MA: D. C. Heath & Co.

Mbanefoh, G.F. 1986. 'Military Presence and the Future of Nigerian Fiscal Federalism'. Ibadan: Faculty of the Social Sciences Lecture Series, No. 1, University of Ibadan.

Mbanefoh, G. and F. Egwaikhide. 1998. 'Revenue Allocation in Nigeria: Derivation Principle Revisited'. In K. Amuwo, A. Agbaje, R. Suberu and G. Herault, eds., *Federalism and Political Restructuring in Nigeria*, 213–231. Ibadan: Spectrum and IFRA.

Obi, C. 1998. 'The Impact of Oil on Nigeria's Revenue Allocation System: Problems and Prospects for National Reconstruction'. In K. Amuwo, A. Agbaje, R. Suberu and G. Herault, eds., *Federalism and Political Restructuring in Nigeria*, 261–275. Ibadan: Spectrum and IFRA.

Odion, L.U. Essien, S. Ajayi and S. Momodu. 2001. 'How Do Oil Governors Spend Their Money?' *ThisDay* (Lagos), June 2:10–12.

Okigbo, P. 1960. 'Nigerian National Accounts'. Paper presented at the International Association for Research in Income and Wealth African Conference, Addis Ababa, January 4–11.

————. 1962. *Nigerian National Accounts, 1950–57.* Lagos: Federal Ministry of Economic Development.

————. 1965a. *Nigerian Public Finance.* Evanston: Northwestern University Press.

————. 1965b. 'Saving and Investment through Government Budgets'. Paper presented at the Rehovoth Conference on Fiscal and Monetary Problems in Developing States, Weizmann Institute of Science, Hebrew University, Jerusalem, August 9–18.

————. 1981. *Nigeria's Financial System: Structure and Growth*. Lagos: Longman.

————. 1983. 'Planning the Nigerian Economy for Less Dependence on Oil'. Distinguished Lecture Series, No. 3. Ibadan: Nigerian Institute of Social and Economic Research.

————. 1993a. *Essays in the Public Philosophy of Development*. Vol. 2. Enugu: Fourth Dimension.

————. 1993b. *Essays in the Public Philosophy of Development*. Vol. 3, Enugu: Fourth Dimension.

Oladeji, Bayo, and Jacob S. Olatunji. 2001. 'Akanbi Panel Probes Ibori, Kure'. *Saturday Tribune* (Ibadan) , June 2:1, 5.

Olowononi, G.D. 1998. 'Revenue Allocation and Economics of Federalism'. In K. Amuwo, A. Agbaje, R. Suberu and G. Herault, eds., *Federalism and Political Restructuring in Nigeria*, 247–260. Ibadan: Spectrum and IFRA.

Onimode, B. 2001. 'How 23 Nations Control their Resources: Case Studies for Nigeria'. *Sunday Tribune* (Ibadan), April 8:9, 11, 16.

Phillips, A. 1971. 'Nigeria's Federal Financial Experience'. *Journal of Modern African Studies* 9(3):389–408.

————. 1976. 'Reforming Nigeria's Revenue Allocation System'. *Nigerian Journal of Public Affairs* 6(1):79–94.

————. 1980. 'Three Decades of Inter-Governmental Financial Relationship in the Federation of Nigeria'. *Quarterly Journal of Administration* 14(2):157–178.

————. 1981. 'From a Service State to a Paternal State'. Inaugural Lecture, University of Ibadan.

Phillipson, S. 1948. *Administrative and Financial Procedure under the New Constitution*. Lagos: Government Printer.

Sagay, Itse. 2001a. 'Nigeria: Federalism, the Constitution and Resource Control (1)'. *Guardian* (Lagos), May 23:4.

————. 2001b. 'Nigeria: Federalism, the Constitution and Resource Control (2)'. *Guardian* (Lagos), May 24:8–9.

————. 2001c. 'Nigeria: Federalism, the Constitution and Resource Control (3)'. *Guardian* (Lagos), May 25:7–8.

Salami, S. 2000. 'Fiscal Tardiness'. *TheNews* (Lagos), October 9:14, 16.

Suberu, R. 1999. 'Integration and Disintegration in the Nigerian Federation'. in D.C. Bach, ed.; *Regionalization in Africa: Integration and Disintegration*, 91–101. Oxford: James Currey.

Suberu, R., and A. Agbaje. 1998. 'The Future of Nigeria's Federalism'. In K. Amuwo, A, Agbaje, R. Suberu and G. Herault, eds., *Federalism and Political Restructuring in Nigeria*, 335–349. Ibadan: Spectrum and IFRA.

Tamuno, T. 1970. 'Separatist Agitations in Nigeria since 1914'. *Journal of Modern African Studies*, 8(4):563–584.

————. 1998. 'Nigerian Federalism in Historical Perspective'. In K. Amuwo, A. Agbaje, R. Suberu and G. Herault, eds., *Federalism and Political Restructuring in Nigeria*, 13–33. Ibadan: Spectrum and IFRA.

Tobi, D. 1989. 'Intergovernmental Fiscal Relations and the Public Policy Process in Nigeria'. In A. Gboyega, Y. Abubakar and Y. Aliyu, eds., *Nigeria since Independence: The First 25 Years*, Vol. 8: *Public Administration*, 126–158. Ibadan: Heinemann Educational Books.

Wildasin, D.E., ed. 1997. *Fiscal Aspects of Evolving Federations*. Cambridge: Cambridge University Press.

5

THE 'STOLEN' OKIGBO PANEL REPORT: OF MALFEASANCE AND PUBLIC ACCOUNTABILITY IN NIGERIA

Pita Ogaba Agbese

Probe! Probe!! Probe!!! That indeed, is the new-found song of Nigeria's ruling regime. After General Sani Abacha effortlessly eased himself into power last November 17, his deputy, Lieutenant-General Oladipo Diya had drummed to the entire nation that their toddling government would not dilly-dally executing probes on the conduct of former public officers. Rather, it would busy itself on addressing subsequent acts of corruption and seeking solutions to daunting and more demanding problems of national prosperity. Quite intriguing is the swiftness with which the Abacha regime is now instituting panels after panels.
— Theophilus Ejorh, 'Season of Inquest', *The African Guardian*, January 17, 1994, 13.

Erring and not betraying public trust and abiding by the requirements of accountability are standards every Nigerian has sought to be judged on. They are conventions ostensibly enshrined in our constitutions... There is even a Code of Conduct Bureau to see to it that the oaths are kept. But the evidence is that the oaths are observed in the breach.
— Chukwuemeka Gahia, 'Code of Conduct', *Newswatch*, January 16, 1995, 8.

INTRODUCTION

On January 19, 1994, General Sani Abacha, the head of state of Nigeria, set up a panel under the chairmanship of the distinguished economist, Pius Okigbo, to reform and reorganize the Central Bank of Nigeria (CBN). The panel undertook an exhaustive and comprehensive examination of the apex bank and issued a report of 'over a hundred thousand words' to the Abacha regime (Okigbo 1994). The panel's voluminous report detailed its findings on the bank and its management of the Nigerian economy. Specifically, the panel examined the role and independence of the bank; the funding of government deficits; the management of domestic and external debt and the foreign exchange regime; the use of the dedication and other special accounts; the internal structure and organization of the bank; the quality of its operations as a banker of last resort, as [a] banker to the government and as [a] regulator of the financial system (Okigbo 1994).

It made numerous recommendations on how to reorganize and restructure the institution to make it more efficient and more effective in discharging its responsibilities. The panel was unsparing in its condemnation of how poorly the bank had run the financial sector of the Nigerian economy. It was very critical of the wanton disregard for laws and regulation that the bank had exhibited in the way it operated. Why did the Abacha junta set up the Okigbo panel? Was this a hidden agenda of the regime to unearth financial misdeeds perpetrated by its predecessor regimes so as to provide legitimacy for its overthrow of the Interim National Government (ING)? How useful are such panels in creating a framework for probity and public accountability in the country? What does a government such as Abacha's gain by instituting public investigation panels? What purpose is served by investing commissions of public inquiry with the stature of eminent Nigerians such as Okigbo? What factors explain the apparent public clamour for commissions of inquiry in the country?

Using the Okigbo panel as a case study, this chapter examines the limits and possibilities of panels of inquiry as a tool for ensuring public accountability and probity in Nigeria. It examines the rationales and the contexts behind the frequent recourse to commissions of inquiry as a strategy for dealing with public malfeasance, corruption and mismanagement in the country. Moreover, this chapter also explores the political strategy of reports of commissions or panels of inquiry. The author argues that investigative panels have not been used as effective checks on the misuse of power in Nigeria. Instead of using such panels or commissions to hold public officials and institutions accountable for their use of public resources, they are mainly used to conduct witch-hunts against political opponents and as substitutes for dealing with difficult political problems. Further, it appears that the Abacha regime's fundamental intention in setting up the Okigbo and other panels was to expose corruption and misdeeds under General Ibrahim Babangida's regime as a justification for Abacha's usurpation of power. Since Abacha himself was highly implicated in many actions of the Babangida regime, however, there were severe limits to which his regime could expose public malfeasance. Accordingly, despite the public fanfare attending the establishment of these panels of inquiry, their findings were often not made public and so remain largely unknown to the vast majority of the Nigerian people several years after the panels were set up.[1] This chapter is divided into four sections. Section one examines the annulment of the June 1993 presidential election and the ousting of the ING as the fundamental backdrop to the setting up of the Okigbo panel. Section two analyzes the panel and its recommendations. The third section reviews the history of public inquiries in Nigeria and a concluding section examines the political uses to which public inquiries are put in Nigeria.

BACKGROUND TO THE OKIGBO PANEL

General Abacha came to power in November 1993 after ousting the ING headed by Ernest Shonekan. The ING was set up by the Babangida regime after it deliberately sabotaged its own programme of transition to civil rule. Babangida himself came to power in August 1985 with a purported grand vision to transform Nigerian politics, economy and society (Babangida c.1989). Several years of a tortuous transition-to-civil-rule programme under the Babangida regime culminated in its annulment of the 1993 presidential election, which was supposed to be the last step in the transition programme. Even though the election was generally acclaimed as free and fair, the Babangida regime annulled it and abrogated the entire transition programme (Omoruyi 1999). A political stalemate created by the annulment forced General Babangida to 'step aside' in August 1993 (Federal Ministry of Information and Culture, n.d.). Shonekan, chairman of the Transitional Council that Babangida had set up in January 1993, was appointed the head of the ING, which was hurriedly cobbled together by Babangida in lieu of relinquishing power to Moshood Abiola who had apparently won the presidential election. In November 1993, a military coup organized by Abacha overthrew the Shonekan-led government (Babangida c.1989).

Babangida's annulment of the 1993 presidential election precipitated a major crisis for the nation. The military's perfidy in annulling the election and truncating the transition programme convinced many Nigerians that the military had no viable solution to the country's nagging problems. Moreover, the brazen manner with which military officers and their civilian collaborators were looting the public treasury, coupled with the virtual collapse of public institutions during the Babangida regime, served as clear proof to many people that military rule had become an unmitigated disaster for the country. The monumental failures of the Babangida regime and the sociopolitical tensions created by military rule threatened the already fragile

---

[1] It should be noted that I had intended to base my analysis in this chapter on a copy of the Okigbo Report, which was 'stolen' by *Newswatch*. In the end, even that copy could not be located.

basis of Nigerian unity. In addition, popular opinion in Nigeria held that ineptness, maladministration, corruption and other observed failures were not unique to the Babangida regime. Rather, they were symptomatic or emblematic of the decades of military rule in Nigeria. Abacha's move in ousting the ING did not dampen the clamour for an end to military rule. Abacha arrested and detained Abiola after Abiola, acting on the basis of his apparent electoral victory, declared himself president of Nigeria. Abacha's incarceration of Abiola, however, did not end the vocal agitation that Abiola must assume office as the elected president. Rather, Abacha's attempt to nullify Abiola's claim to the presidency only served to heighten the public demand for an end to military rule. Therefore, it was within the context of establishing legitimacy for itself that the Abacha regime set up the Okigbo and other panels of inquiry. Although many of these panels and other commissions of inquiry had been set up before Abiola's incarceration, it was clear that Abacha was profoundly concerned about the legitimacy of his regime in the face of the overwhelming electoral success recorded by Abiola during the June 1993 election. Despite initial statements by General Diya (as shown in the opening quotation) that the regime would not probe former office holders, Abacha's acute awareness of the unease and suspicion caused by his coup is betrayed in his maiden broadcast as head of state. He stated:

> Many have expressed fears about the apparent return of the military. Many have talked about the concern of the international community. However, under the present circumstances the survival of our beloved country is far above every other consideration. Nigeria is the only country we have. We must, therefore, solve our problems ourselves. We must lay a very solid foundation for the growth of true democracy. We should avoid any ad hoc or temporary solutions. The problems must be addressed firmly, objectively, decisively and with all sincerity of purpose (Abacha, November 18, 1993).

THE OKIGBO PANEL AND ITS RECOMMENDATIONS
Certain facts about contemporary Nigerian politics and economy are not in dispute. First, since the 1970s, revenues from the sale of crude oil have provided the vibrancy behind most economic activities. The bulk of government revenues and export earnings are derived from petroleum exports. Second, the country has earned a substantial amount of money from crude oil sales over the past three decades. One estimate is that over $280 billion have accrued to Nigeria from oil exports within this period. Third, most of these revenues have been spent, with very little accountability to the Nigerian public, by successive governments over the years. Fourth, intense

political struggles over state power in the country have largely revolved around the desire to control the enormous amounts of money that flow into government coffers from petroleum exports. For instance, from 1966 until 1999, there were eight coups and coup attempts as various factions in the armed forces jostled for state power. Guns and money have served as veritable tools for the acquisition of power in Nigeria. Fifth, the relative ease with which the state earns the oil revenues coupled with the absence of accountability on how the money is expended have created numerous avenues for government officials and their collaborators to amass stupendous amounts of the oil money to themselves through corruption. Finally, substantial environmental degradation has resulted from oil exploration, production and transportation of oil. Most Nigerians who live in the oil-producing areas derive no benefits from oil exports. When their abject poverty and the despoliation of their environment are juxtaposed against the luxury bought with the stupendous amounts of money that corrupt top government officials appropriate to themselves, it is easy to understand the ferocity and militancy with which Nigerians in the Niger Delta now demand local ownership and control of petroleum resources.

The Okigbo panel was part of a series of panels set up by the Abacha regime to investigate various institutions. The General Emmanuel Abisoye panel was set up to scrutinize the Nigerian National Petroleum Corporation (NNPC). Another panel, headed by Justice Kayode Esho, was set up to investigate the judiciary and identify the problems existing in the country's legal system. Yet another panel was mandated to probe allegations of corruption against the military administrators of Osun, Borno, Yobe, Kano and Sokoto states. Moreover, a number of audit committees were set up to review financial procedures in the federal ministries and the National Electric Power Authority (NEPA). At one level, we can view the formation of the Okigbo panel as a fulfilment of the promise made by General Abacha when he came to power in his first broadcast on November 28, 1993 when he promised full-scale 're-organization and reform' in the police, customs, the judiciary, NITEL, NNPC, NEPA, the banking industry and higher educational institutions.

Several other antecedents compelled the Abacha regime to institute the Okigbo panel. First, a 1993 World Bank report noted out that the Nigerian government could not account for $3 billion in Gulf War oil sales proceeds. Second, in June 1991, William Keeling, the Lagos correspondent of the *Financial Times* in London, had been deported from Nigeria for his report that more than half of the oil money earned during the Gulf War had been spent on the Liberian peacekeeping operation, the Organization of African Unity's summit at Abuja and the aluminium smelter at Ikot Abasi (*Financial*

Times, June 27, 1991, 4). While Keeling claimed that Nigeria earned approximately 50 billion naira as Gulf War windfall and had spent about 30 billion naira, the federal government claimed that it had earned only 20.2 billion naira as windfall and had spent only 5 billion naira of this sum on debt-servicing. In response to Keeling's publication, the federal government maintained that it wished to:

> ...state categorically that the estimates of 'oil windfall' contained in Keeling's story are without any foundation and that the additional proceeds realized from the sale of oil during the Gulf crisis have largely been saved, and were not utilized to finance any of the projects referred to in the publication. In fact, given the painful experience that the country suffered in the past, when periods of relatively buoyant foreign earnings were quickly followed by acute shortages, resulting in severe set-backs to the country's development efforts, Government deliberately decided the last time around not to let the temporary windfall affect normal expenditure patterns and raise hopes and aspirations that cannot be sustained (*Citizen*, July 8, 1991, 16–17).

Third, the Budget Monitoring Committee, headed by Clement Isong, which submitted its report in August 1993, had called for an inquiry into the $1.5 billion of revenue paid into off-budgetary special accounts (dedicated accounts) within the first six months of 1993. Fourth, reckless spending under the Babangida regime convinced many Nigerians that public resources had been wasted and misappropriated. During the hearings of the Abisoye panel, General Abacha himself observed:

> In the past decade or so, there had arisen a situation whereby the average Nigerian could legitimately wonder and complain as to why his country's earnings have not been reflected adequately in the well-being of our teeming populace. In a sense, our people with some justification feel outraged and short-changed by what they regard as persistent and massive leakage of our country's external earnings (Abacha, 1994, 6).

There was therefore, the need to authenticate the suspicion about illegitimate appropriation of money by senior government officials.

After seven months of intense scrutiny of the Central Bank, the Okigbo panel made a number of important findings. First, it noted that although Decree No. 24 of 1991 granted the bank autonomy from the Federal Ministry of Finance, it placed the bank directly under the presidency. This, the panel discovered, did not give the bank sufficient autonomy to act independently of the government. To remedy this, the panel made three recommendations designed to ensure the bank's autonomy. First, it recommended that the position of the governor should be insulated through his appointment by the president subject to confirmation by the senate. Second, it suggested the formation of a financial services coordinating committee that would be headed by the governor of the CBN to coordinate the activities of the eight apex regulatory agencies in the financial system. Third, it recommended the immediate establishment of a committee on fiscal and monetary policy, to be chaired by the vice-president with a membership composed of the governor of the CBN, the economic adviser and ministers of finance, national planning and petroleum resources.

In addition, the Okigbo panel observed that the law required that the CBN not advance more than 12.5 percent of the budgeted revenue for each year, yet for seven/eight years, it had advanced more than 50 percent. The panel observed that 'on no account must the governor either be made or allowed to break the law. His position as governor should be on the line should the bank exceed the 12.5 percent limit'. It stressed that breaking the law was sufficient ground to remove the bank's governor from office.

Lastly, the panel expressed alarm concerning the management of Nigeria's external debt. Okigbo (1994) noted in a speech during his submission of the panel's report that:

...our annual external debt service now runs at over four percent of the GDP; add to this our postulated population growth rate of 2.5 percent. It therefore follows that, to achieve the slightest improvement in the lives of our common folk, Nigeria must grow at a minimum of 6.5 percent per annum in real terms on a sustainable basis. The moral imperative of this is that anyone with the responsibility for the welfare of his country would do well to hurry up to seek genuine debt relief on concessionary terms. But these reliefs are available only for those with a prudent and realistic program of economic management that encourages improved earnings of foreign resources, reduced import demand and judicious use and application of resources to productive purposes (Okigbo 1994).

In its report, the panel issued several important findings on the dedicated accounts that had been created by the Babangida regime. The first of these was created in 1986 with the allocation of 20,000 barrels of crude oil per day to finance the liquefied natural gas (LNG) project. The logic behind the establishment of this account was that the LNG was a priority project that should not compete with other programmes for the allocation of expenditures. In

April 1988, more dedicated accounts were opened with a commitment of 50,000 barrels a day. Unanticipated windfall oil revenue from the 1990 Gulf War was also deposited in a special account. By 1993, the number of projects financed from such special and dedicated accounts had grown to six with an allocation of about 105,000 barrels a day of crude petroleum (see Tables 5.1–5.5 for listings of the dedicated accounts and the patterns of expenditures). Table 5.1 shows the receipts and disbursements attributed to these accounts between 1988 and 1994. Throughout, the ostensible rationale governing the creation of the special and dedicated accounts was that in this way the federal government would guarantee that oil profits would finance projects critical to the health of the economy. The federal government also stressed that such dedicated allotments would be used exclusively for such projects; however, the level of financial malfeasance connected with these projects was enormous. From the president himself to the governors to other officers, federal officials at all levels were dipping their hands into these accounts for expenses not at all connected with the special projects. Neither the president nor the governor accounted to anyone for these massive extra-budgetary expenditures.

The Okigbo panel discovered that of the total amount of $12.4 billion deposited in dedicated accounts from 1988 to 1994, $12.2 billion had been spent in only six years on 'what could neither be adjudged genuine high priority nor truly regenerative investment'. It observed that neither the president nor the governor of the Central Bank accounted to anyone for the expenditures. Furthermore, the panel decried the situation in which huge 'expenditures were clandestinely undertaken while the country was openly reeling with a crushing external debt overhang', arguing that this represented 'a gross abuse of public trust'. Okigbo noted that had the $12.4 billion, or even a significant proportion had been paid into the external reserves, 'the impact on the naira/dollar exchange rate today; on the attitude of our external creditors; on the credibility of Nigeria and on the environment for foreign investment, etc. would have been incalculable' (Okigbo 1994, 8).

It was clear that the dedicated accounts had become conduits for massive corruption. For instance, *Newswatch* investigations showed that if money from the dedicated account was needed for any undertaking, a note was sent by Abdulkadir Ahmed to the CBN's director of foreign operations stating that he should release so many million dollars for a designated project. It would then be directed that the note should stand as a directive and a receipt for such money. In all cases, the accounts were debited accordingly. CBN sources said that the bank did not request, demand, or receive any documentary evidence of the services or projects paid for because these were deemed classified (*Newswatch*, January 16, 1995, 12). It was also evident as shown in Tables 5.2, 5.3, 5.4 and 5.5 that some of the expenditures from the dedicated accounts were of a frivolous nature. This and the alarming abuse to which the accounts were put compelled the Okigbo panel to recommend their immediate closure, with the remaining balance transferred to the nation's external reserves. Regarding fraudulent practices, the Okigbo panel declared:

> We are pleasantly astonished at the relatively few cases of successfully perpetrated fraud within the bank. We are alarmed at the very large number of cases reported by the bank to the police for investigation and prosecution but which, even after six to seven years, have not gone beyond the stage of police investigation. We are frightened by the countless number of '419' cases around the bank and often involving the name of the bank and amounting to scores of billions of dollars. These cases are fully documented and reported to the police. The fault, we are constrained to say, is not so much with the bank as with the system of crime investigation and law enforcement in which the bank finds itself (Okigbo 1994).

In its recommendations concerning the structure and operation of the bank, the panel observed that the more junior members of the professional staff possessed higher standards or qualifications than many of the senior staff, noting that an unduly large proportion of the senior staff with more than ten years' service were intellectually and technically weak. Thus, it urged that the bank undertake drastic cutbacks to eliminate incompetent staff to ensure that its policy-making capacity would not be handicapped or obstructed (Okigbo 1994).

Table 5.1
Special and Dedication Accounts: Receipts and Disbursements, 1988–June 1994 (US$)

Type of Account	Receipts	Disbursements	Balance
Dedication	6,195,381,252.42	6,109,437,372.97	85,943,879.45
Sale (Mining Rights)	1,747,504,435.83	1,745,841,416.91	1,663,018.92
Signature Bonus	100,069,668.33	99,000,000.00	1,069,668.33
Stabilization Fund	4,398,610,482.36	4,281,250,046.02	117,360,434.34
Total	12,441,565,838.94	12,235,528,835.90	206,037,001.04

Source: Aina 1995, 10.

64   Vision and Policy in Nigerian Economics

Table 5.2
Revenues Accruing to Dedication and other Special Accounts, 1988–1994 ($million)

Year	Dedication Accounts	Sale of Mining Rights	Signature Bonus	Stabilization
1988	$ 232.4	–	–	–
1989	459.8	$1,525.60	–	–
1990	757.7	100.30	–	$1,234.30
1991	1,033.9	69.96	–	1,160.80
1992	1,581.4	49.94	–	1,922.40
1993	1,631.0	1,639.45	100.05	9.16
1994	499.2	27.18	17.48	1.97

Source: Aina 1995, 10.

Table 5.3
Selected Expenditures of Dedication Account ($million)

Item	Amount
Nigerian High Commission, UK	$ 18.12
Nigerian Embassy, Saudi Arabia	14.99
Nigerian Embassy, Iran	2.76
Nigerian Embassy, Niger	3.80
Nigerian Embassy, Pakistan	3.80
Nigerian Embassy, Israel	13.07
Ministry of Defence	323.35
Security	59.72
Defence Attachés	25.49
Documentary film on Nigeria	2.92
TV/Video for the presidency	18.30
Ceremonial Uniform (Army)	3.85
Staff Welfare (Dodan Barracks/Aso Rock	23.98
President's overseas travel	8.95
First Lady's overseas travels	0.99
Medical Equipment for Aso Rock	27.25

Source: Aina 1995, 10.

Table 5.4
Expenditure of Dedication Account on Projects (Amount in $million)

Year	Abuja	Ajaokuta	Ikot Abasi	Itakpe	Shiroro	Others	Total
1988	–	47.07	–	27.62	0.38	8.45	83.51
1989	39.01	240.81	119.48	46.68	37.49	9.54	493.01
1990	115.38	366.10	138.67	74.31	14.22	89.94	798.62
1991	733.87	373.01	224.04	275.39	2.49	111.84	1,720.64
1992	435.62	297.39	198.57	280.33	32.61	280.89	1,525.41
1993	131.85	148.87	84.70	100.33	3.86	140.02	609.63
1994	62.73	0.00	0.00	0.16	0.00	10.67	73.56
Total	1,518.47	1,473.24	765.45	804.81	91.05	651.34	5,304.37

Source: Aina 1995, 12.

Table 5.5
Disbursements from the Dedication Account (1988–1994) ($million)

Year	Projects	Presidency	Defence	Security	Others	Total
1988	83.51	6.00	–	–	–	89.51
1989	493.01	11.81	44.76	19.06	–	568.64
1990	798.62	52.33	58.80	0.41	–	910.16
1991	1,720.64	40.66	27.30	9.48	–	1,798.07
1992	1,525.41	102.41	134.84	12.25	–	1,774.90
1993	609.63	49.36	89.98	66.71	8.97	824.66
1994	73.56	–	45.56	22.86	1.50	143.50
Total	5,304.37	262.57	401.23	130.77	10.50	6,109.44

Source: Aina 1995, 13.

Moreover, the panel was also concerned about the technological weakness of the bank. According to Okigbo, a significant number of staff resisted modern technology whereas they ought to embrace it. The bank had scandalously wasted a lot of money in the fruitless and uncoordinated pursuit of computerization since 1976. Ironically, instead of the CBN providing leadership in the use of information technology within the financial services industry, it was more backward than the financial institutions it was expected to examine and supervise (Okigbo 1994, 2). In his final eloquent state-ment, Okigbo cautiously concluded that the mission of the panel was:

...[to] deliver a bank worthy of the country, alive to its responsibilities and well equipped to discharge them without fear. We have provided a trimmer and slimmer bank that, assisted with modern information technology and greater work ethic, should now be morally propelled to a higher standard of professional services. How far it will succeed will depend ultimately on how much the government will leave it alone to discharge its statutory functions and responsibilities in accordance with its professional norms and etiquette. The implementation of our recommendations must be entrusted to people, both within and outside the bank, who recognize the dangers ahead and who have nothing to gain from frustrating the institution or perverting its ethos. We have fulfilled our own part of the bargain to produce a report. Your Excellency's part is to shorten its shelf life to the absolute minimum and to pull our recommendations quickly into the mainstream of policy (Okigbo 1994, 2).

A BRIEF HISTORY OF COMMISSIONS OF INQUIRY IN NIGERIA

Although the military has made commissions of inquiry a ubiquitous feature of the Nigerian political landscape, such commissions predated military rule.

During the colonial era, commissions were often used to deal with difficult political issues. For instance, in September 1957, the Colonial Office appointed the Henry Willink Commission to 'enquire into the fears of Minorities and the means of allaying them' (United Kingdom, Colonial Office, Nigeria 1958, 4). Numerous panels of inquiry had investigated abuse of office by public holders during and after colonial rule; however, the military claimed that the nefarious activities of civilian political leaders compelled it to intervene in politics. Thus, the appointment of commissions of inquiry became an article of faith in military governance in Nigeria and a means of legitimizing its takeover of the government.

After General Gowon was ousted as head of state in 1975, his successor, General Murtala Mohammed, instituted several panels to investigate military governors and other public office holders under the Gowon regime. Out of the then twelve military governors, ten were found guilty of corrupt enrichment and they were dismissed from the police and the armed forces and ordered to forfeit the money and other property they had illegally acquired. Interestingly, this action demonstrated the military that had come to power to rid Nigeria of corruption and abuse of power had itself become implicated in public malfeasance. The next wholesale use of panels of inquiry occurred after Major-General Muhammadu Buhari led a successful coup against Shehu Shagari's regime in December 1983. Widespread beliefs about the profligate corruption of civilian politicians under the Shagari administration were buttressed by revelations of prebendalism on a massive scale. General Buhari set up special military tribunals to try hundreds of politicians for 'corruption and abuse of office'.[2] In the ensuing trials, incredible revelations of corruption, graft and embezzlement of hundreds of millions of naira were made (Federal Government of Nigeria 1986a; 1986b, 5). Many politicians were found guilty and sentenced to long jail terms. For instance, Jim Nwobodo, former governor of Anambra State, was convicted of corrupt enrichment and sentenced to twenty-two years in jail on each of twelve counts of wrongdoing. (Oluojede 1986, 20). Convicted politicians were also required to refund to the state millions of naira or return illegally acquired property that they illegally appropriated while in power.

By the time that the Buhari regime was itself overthrown in August 1985, many of the arrested politicians had not yet been tried, even though they had already spent over seventeen months in detention. Accordingly, one of the first acts of the Babangida regime was to set up new panels to review

---

[2] A special decree, Recovery of Public Property (Special Military Tribunals Decree, No. 3, 1984, was promulgated and was used to prosecute many of the ousted politicians. For details of this decree, see Federal Republic of Nigeria, *Official Gazette (Extraordinary)* March 19, 1984, A29–A52.

the cases of the politicians who had already been sentenced and to prosecute politicians who had not yet been tried. Perhaps the two most important of these were the Justice Mohammed Bello Judicial Tribunal and the Justice Uwaifo Judicial Tribunal. The Bello Tribunal's mandate was to review the cases of politicians who had already been tried and convicted. It affirmed that most of the politicians had been properly convicted by the military tribunals, though in many cases, it recommended lighter jail terms than those that had been imposed. In addition, the Bello Tribunal recommended that politicians found guilty be barred from holding public posts. The government fully accepted this recommendation (Federal Republic of Nigeria 1986a, 8). The Uwaifo Tribunal, on the other hand, was established to prosecute politicians and other public officers whose cases had not come before the Buhari military tribunals. It convicted many accused politicians.

Later, the ban imposed on the basis of the report of the Bello Tribunal was enlarged to include not just politicians convicted of wrongdoing, but all politicians. In a television broadcast on June 16, 1986, Babangida declared that: 'all past politicians are hereby banned from seeking or holding any public office for ten years... They may vote; but they cannot be voted for. In addition, they must not be involved in any overt or covert political party or partisan activities' (see broadcast text, 9). In effect, the sins of corrupt and convicted politicians were visited on all politicians by collectively precluding them from further participation in politics. This blanket ban order was later amended and codified in the Participation in Politics and Elections (Prohibition) Decree No. 25 (1987). Under its terms, any Nigerian who had ever been (or would ever be) convicted of corruption or other official misdeeds was banned for life from 'holding any elective office or post, public office, political party office, whether elective or otherwise either in the government or in any political party'.

Moreover, the Political Bureau, established by the Babangida regime to ascertain the type of political system most conducive to Nigeria, recommended that convicted politicians as well as certain designated politicians of the First and Second Republics be disqualified from participating in the politics of the Third Republic (Federal Republic of Nigeria, 1987). It argued that democratic stability in Nigeria could only be attained with the institutionalization of a new political order, pointing out that the new political order must be built on a high standard of morality and a new and wholesome attitude to public office. According to the bureau, the politicians of the two previous republics had failed to establish the high moral standards demanded by a new political order. Accordingly, they must yield to a new breed of politician (Federal Government of Nigeria 1987, 218).

Decree 25 was, among other reasons, enacted both as a punitive and as a socially redemptive measure. The assumption was that a public officer who betrayed public trust through corrupt enrichment must be punished for such betrayal by depriving him of the opportunity of holding any public office. The Bello Tribunal white paper eloquently expressed this reasoning when it proclaimed that:

> Government is of the firm belief that public office holding is a public trust, and therefore anybody who abuses this public trust must be disqualified from holding public office either for a specific period of time or for the rest of his life as deemed appropriate in order, firstly, to ensure that he does not have another opportunity for such misconduct and secondly, to serve as an object lesson to others who might be tempted in like manner.

POLITICAL USES OF INVESTIGATIVE PANELS

As is clear from the preceding discussion, investigative panels serve to discredit politicians while at the same time, create a basis for legitimizing military rule in general. Given the high propensity for military officers to engage in corrupt practices, however, the appointment of panels of inquiry was also deployed by factions within the military in internecine struggles for the acquisition of political power. Thus, an anticorruption crusade manifested by the appointment of panels of inquiry becomes an important strategy by which one faction of the military discredits another so as to establish its own legitimacy to rule in place of the ousted faction.

It can be argued that the rationale that underpinned military intervention in Nigerian politics compelled the establishment of commissions of inquiry by successive military regimes. From the first military coup in January 1966, military incursions into politics had rested on the claim that the military intervened to rid the society of corruption and other forms of public malfeasance. In other words, the honour and credibility of military regimes depended on their noisy wars against corruption. As Bala J. Takaya (1989, 73) has rightly noted, 'most public servants measure success in terms of material possessions accumulated while in public office'. It is quite common in many political systems for the government to appoint an administrative review commission to assess the administrative structure of a public institution and to recommend ways of reforming such structures to make them perform better. An excellent example of this in Nigeria was the 1974 Jerome Udoji Civil Service Review Commission (Federal Republic of Nigeria 1974, 4). Its two major terms of reference were:

1. to examine the organization, structure and management of the public services and recommend reforms where desirable; and
2. to investigate and evaluate the methods of recruitment and conditions of employment and the staff development programmes of the public services and to recommend such changes as may be necessary.

The Udoji Commission made a number of recommendations. First, it suggested a 'new conception of management' in the public service that would result in a shift in emphasis to 'production or result-oriented approach' to public service. Second, it urged that attempts be made to recruit and train people with specialized scientific and technical knowledge. Lastly, it recommended improved conditions of service as an incentive for public servants. The findings and recommendations of a fact-finding panel such as Udoji's may serve as an important guide to subsequent public policy. A government may betray its preferred policy option by the manner it appoints such a commission. As Umar Benna (1989, 250) has argued, the selection of the memers of the Committee on the Location of the Federal Capital was designed to ensure a positive outcome towards relocation, thus enhancing the legitimacy of the outcome.

There are other uses for public commissions. They may also function as an effective way of dealing with 'vital and controversial issues'. For in-stance, the Muhammed regime appointed the Committee on Location of the Federal Capital to examine the dual role of Lagos as a federal and state capital and the relocation of the federal capital (Federal Republic of Nigeria, White Paper 1976, 5). A commission of inquiry may review policy and in-vestigate public opinion with a view to avoid inappropriate measures and institute reforms and restructuring of outmoded institutions and policy structures. Many such commissions have been set up in Nigeria in the aftermath of intercommunal or religious conflicts. Alternatively, a public panel of investigation can operate as a strategy by a government to buy time or defer making difficult decisions, a substitute for taking hard political decision. Used nefariously, a commission of inquiry serves as a diversionary tactic for the state. Thus, it can be used as a pretence by an otherwise incompetent administration to pretend that it is responsive to its public. In other words, it can serve as a substitute for real and effective governance.

CONCLUSION

Even though the appointment of panels of inquiry and other administrative commissions has played a significant role in the governance of Nigeria, the impact of such panels or commissions on the conduct of public affairs has been minimal. This is so for a number of reasons. First, in many cases, the government that appoints the panel itself has no moral standing to carry out far-reaching investigations. As Clement Nwankwo (1994) observed with respect to the panels set up by the Abacha regime:

> I am amazed when I hear of probes because corruption is very fundamental in Nigeria and a probe should not be cosmetic. If the government is determined to fight corruption, then it has to go to the basics. There are doubts about the moral credibility of officials in government right from the head of state downwards. There are different stories about Abacha's involvement in business, in land deals. One would hope that if there is going to be a probe, whoever is at the head of government should be seen to be above board or be seen to be ready to have a clean government. Until that is clear, I think perhaps, this probe is only capable of arousing more curiosity. I do not believe that this government has the moral courage to do a thorough probe of those institutions.

Ironically, Abacha, who instituted so many of these panels, turned out to be one of the most corrupt leaders that Nigeria has ever had. After his death in 1998, an enormous number of articles in Nigerian and international newspapers and news magazines have detailed accounts of how Abacha and other members of his family looted the Nigerian treasury (e.g., Olorunfewa 2000, 12–18).

Second, under the military, it was frequently the case that even though a new government was genuinely anxious to probe the activities of the predecessor government, at the same time, it tried to shield itself from public scrutiny. Thus, despite its zealotry in prosecuting ousted politicians, the Buhari regime enacted a decree that shielded the regime from scrutiny. For instance, according to Decree No. 4 of 1984, it was an offence to publish anything (whether true or false) that brought the government or public officer to ridicule or disrepute:

> Any person who publishes in any form, whether written or otherwise, any message, rumour or statement, being a message, rumour, statement or report which is false in any material particular or which brings or is calculated to bring the Federal Military Government or the Government of a State or public officer to ridicule or disrepute, shall be guilty of an offence under this Decree (Supplement to Official Gazette Extraordinary, April 4, 1984, 9).

Chris W. Ogbondah (1994) has argued that Decree 4 was enacted to prevent press insinuations that Buhari was corrupt.

Third, the sheer number of panels and commissions that have been set up in Nigeria creates the impression that public accountability is entrenched in the Nigerian political system. On the contrary, the proliferation of probe panels and commissions with their ad hoc nature betray the fact that public accountability.has not been successfully institutionalized in the country. Public inquiries in the mould favoured by military rulers in Nigeria tended to have obfuscated rather than illuminated important political issues. While the commissions created the appearance that Nigerian military regimes were serious about public accountability, it was clear that the military regimes never raised fundamental questions on public accountability in the country. Yusufu Bala Usman has raised a few such questions:

> Is the purpose of public accountability essentially to prevent agitation and protest and keep the public quiet and pacified? Or is the purpose to make the public understand what the leaders are doing for them so that they can more effectively follow and submit? Or is the purpose essentially to render account in the sense of profit or loss of public revenue? Or is the purpose of public accountability to enable the public control the goals, nature, methods and operations of a political system on a permanent basis through a continuous flow of information, discussion and decision in popular organs? (Usman 1979, 112).

Usman (1979, 113) has made a very important observation that a public which consists essentially of peasant farmers and wage-earners cannot make a leadership, or indeed anybody, accountable to it in a society built on the private ownership and accumulation of wealth; especially a society in which this private accumulation by a tiny minority is carried on almost entirely through the manipulation of public office and institutions. Thus, under military rule in Nigeria, public inquests became a 'tacit diversionary tactic, a smokescreen that is only aimed at deflecting public mind from more crucial and urgent matters of state, and indeed to mask the various inadequacies and perhaps certain suspicions of the government'.

Another fundamental problem with panels of inquiry in Nigeria is that ultimately they promise much and deliver very little. While they are anchored in public accountability, real public accountability has no place for military intervention in politics! There is no room for military usurpation of power where public accountability has become the norm of society. Illegal acquisition of political power symbolized by military coups constitutes the ultimate form of indiscipline; it is the negation of public accountability.

Thus, the military promises what it does not possess and cannot give. It cannot offer accountability because it is the lack of public accountability that justifies military intervention in civilian politics in the first place. As the Nigerian case has amply demonstrated, even after military regimes had gone through the charade of appointing panels of inquiry, they lacked the moral or political courage to release the findings. Thus, despite Okigbo's pleas that the Abacha regime should 'shorten the shelf life' of his panel's report to the 'absolute minimum', that report has still not been released seven years after it was submitted to the government. There is also a beguiling quality that makes such panels ultimately politically dangerous. They tend to contribute to political helplessness and ennui of the Nigerian masses by turning them into mere spectators in their own affairs. Panels are set up within the context in which the public believes that top political leaders use their official positions to amass wealth at the expense of the public. The amassed evidence augments this belief. Although the public's hunger for accountability is genuine, the strategy of using panels as a substitute for accountability becomes a charade that ultimately deepens political cynicism. In the end, the superficiality of panels leaves the public more disillusioned about the nature and purpose of the state and the leadership. This is made even more glaring in instances in which former government officials, who had been convicted of corrupt enrichment, are subsequently pardoned and rehabilitated. For instance, all the military governors, who were convicted by the Murtala Muhammed regime and stripped of their ill-gotten gains, were rehabilitated by the Babangida regime and their confiscated properties returned to them.

Yet at another level, the establishment of panels of inquiry, many of which are chaired by academics, raises questions about the role of intellectuals in Nigeria. Attahiru Jega has raised a number of important questions. He asks:

To what extent are [intellectuals] the ideologues of hegemonic classes and interests? What is the dividing line between 'neocolonial philistines' and 'revolutionary intellectuals'? At what point do narrow 'class' interests become wedded to wider 'popular' interests when academics confront the State? (Jega 1994, 2).

Similarly, Nigeria's foremost novelist, Chinua Achebe, has argued as follows:

One of the most urgent matters for Nigerians to address when they settle down to debate the national question is the issue of collaboration by professionals and technocrats with corrupt and repressive regimes. We must devise effective sanctions against our lawyers and judges and doctors and university professors who debase their profession in their zealotry to serve as tyranny's errand boys, thus contributing in large measure to the general decay of honesty and integrity in our national life (Achebe 1993, 4).

Military governments in Nigeria used the stature and integrity of eminent scholars such as Okigbo, to give credibility to their panels of inquiry, but in the end, they debased such scholars by not heeding their advice and recommendations. Tributes have been paid to the memory of Okigbo, but no tribute can be more important than the release of the report of the Okigbo panel. This conference being in honour of Pius Okigbo should ask the Obasanjo administration to release the report and thus ensure that Okigbo and his colleagues did not labour in vain.

REFERENCES

Abacha, General Sani. 1993. Broadcast. November 28.
_____. 1994. Speech at the Inauguration of the Abisoye Panel to Probe the Nigerian National Petroleum Corporation, January.
Achebe, Chinua. 1993. 'Anniversary of Regrets'. *The African News Weekly*, October:4.
Aina, Wale Akin. 1995. 'Pandora's Box'. *Newswatch* (Lagos), January 16:9-14.
Babangida, Ibrahim. 1986. Broadcast. June 16.
_____. 1989. *Selected Speeches of IBB*. Ibadan: Precision Press.
Babatope, Ebenezer. 1995. *The Abacha Regime and the June 12 Crisis: A Struggle for Democracy*. Ikeja, Lagos: Ebino Topsy.
Benna, Umar G. 1989. 'The Federal Capital: The Debate and the Planning'. In Tekena Tamuno and J.A. Atanda (eds.), *Nigeria since Independence: The First 25 Years*, Vol.4: *Government and Public Policy*, 247-256 Ibadan: Heinemann Books.
Citizen. 1991. Text of Federal Government's Response to Keeling Report. July 8:16-17.
Federal Republic of Nigeria. 1974. *Main Report of the Public Service Review Commission*. Lagos: Government Printer.
_____. 1976. *White Paper on the Report of the Committee on the Location of the Federal Capital*. Lagos: Government Printer.

_____. 1984a. 'Decree No. 4: Public Officers Protection against False Accusation Decree'. Supplement to Official Gazette Extraordinary, April 4:9.

_____. 1984b. 'Recovery of Public Property (Special Military Tribunals Decree, No. 3, *Official Gazette (Extraordinary)* 71(15), March 19:A29–A52.

_____. 1986a. *Views and Decisions of the Federal Military Government on the Report and Recommendations of the Justice Mohammed Bello Judicial Tribunal to Review Cases of Persons Convicted under Decree No. 3 of 1984.* Lagos: Federal Government Printer.

_____. 1986b. *Views and Decisions of the Federal Military Government on the Report and Recommendations of Justice Uwaifo Special Panel.* Lagos: Government Printer, 1986.

_____. 1987. *Report of the Political Bureau.* Lagos: Government Printer.

Financial Times. 1991. June 27:4.

Great Britain, Colonial Office, Nigeria. 1958. *Report of the Commission Appointed to Enquire into the Fears of Minorities and the Means of Allaying Them.* London: Her Majesty's Stationery Office.

Jega, Attahiru M. 1994. *Nigerian Academics under Military Rule.* Stockholm: University of Stockholm.

Nigeria. Federal Ministry of Information and Culture. n.d. *June 12* and *The Future of Nigerian Democracy.* Lagos: Federal Ministry of Information and Culture.

Nwankwo, Clement. 1994. 'Abacha is in a Glass House'. *African Guardian* (Lagos), January 17:17.

Ogbondah, Chris W. 1994. *Military Regimes and the Press in Nigeria, 1966–1993: Human Rights and National Development.* Lanham: University Press of America.

Olojede, Dele. 1986. 'Save Our Souls'. *Newswatch*, September 15:18–20, 22.

Olorunfewa, Ade. 2000. 'The Wages of Sleaze'. *Tell*, July 24:12–18.

Okigbo, Pius. 1994. 'Abuse of Public Trust', [Excerpts from the statement made by Dr. Okigbo during the submission of the report of the Okigbo panel to General Sani Abacha, August, 1994.] Reproduced in *Newswatch*, October 24:32–33.

Omoruyi, Omo. 1999. *The Tale of June 12: The Betrayal of the Democratic Rights of Nigerians (1993).* London: Press Alliance Network.

Takaya, Bala J. 1989. 'The Nigerian Public Service and Accountability since Independence: Morale, Performance and Probity'. In Alex Gboyega, Yaya Abubakar and Yaya Aliyu, eds., *Nigeria since Independence: The First 25 Years*, Vol. 8: *Public Administration*, 41–60. Ibadan: Heinemann Books.

United Kingdom, Colonial Office, Nigeria. 1958. *Report of the Commission Appointed to Enquire into the Fears of Minorities and the Means of Allaying Them*. London: Her Majesty's Stationery Office.

Usman, Yusufu Bala. 1979. *For the Liberation of Nigeria: Essays and Lectures, 1969–1978*. London: New Beacon Books.

6

OKIGBO AND THE IGBO QUESTION
IN NIGERIAN POLITICS

Ebere Onwudiwe

This chapter focuses on the role of Pius Okigbo during the civil war and after. The first part will zero in on the multipurpose functions he carried out for the state of Biafra and the second part on his leadership role after the war. Okigbo's role in Biafra was multifaceted, involving intellectual, advisory and diplomatic functions. He was one of the main planners in the Biafran think tank that formulated Biafran economic policies, which included contingency plans for Biafra. As a seceding nation, it was necessary for Biafra to have in place complete plans for different scenarios and outcomes. Thus, Okigbo and his team developed contingency plans to serve the Igbo interest along two lines, one in case the war for an independent Biafran state succeeded, and the other for peaceful re-absorption in the case that the Igbo lost the war. These plans were in place prior to the declaration of the state of Biafra.

ROLE DURING THE CIVIL WAR
During the war itself, Okigbo was a prominent member of the Biafran war cabinet. Lieutenant-Colonel (later General) Chukwuemeka Odumegwu Ojukwu deployed him as Biafra's roving ambassador. Whenever crises developed among senior officers on war fronts, Ojukwu often sent him on peace missions to the commanders of those fronts. He generally succeeded in settling conflicts and re-establishing peace among feuding officers. The secret of his success is not hard to find. He enjoyed great respect among the senior officers who had great confidence in his wisdom and impartiality. Ojukwu knew that few Igbo civilians enjoyed the same degree of respect

among military officers, as did Okigbo. Ojukwu valued his ability to make the senior officers toe the line, while the officers knew that Okigbo could ensure that their requests for equipment and other supplies were fulfilled. Okigbo also furthered the Igbo cause in international diplomacy. Often he participated in the secret negotiations that took place between Nigeria and Biafra. Besides these missions, he visited other countries on behalf of Biafra, and it is very likely that his efforts were responsible for Tanzania's decision to recognize Biafra as a state.

In 1970 the Igbo were defeated by the federal army. This very painful situation was aggravated by the fact that the Nigerian government was led by the military regime that fought the Biafran war and was thus still inclined to treat Igbos as enemiès, notwithstanding Gowon's public declarations of 'no victor, no vanquished'. This constituted a very dangerous environment for Igbo leaders, some of whom were imprisoned or had their property seized. Okigbo himself was thrown into jail for close to two years. Many Ndigbo[1] leaders were detained by the military government. But for the brutal presence of the military government, it was a situation perfect for the Igbo psyche: 'no leaders please'. It is widely believed that the Igbo prefer collective leadership rather than one-man leadership. One of the most successful Igbo organizations, the Igbo State Union,[2] was built on this collective structure of political leadership. In fact, today many Nigerians make jokes about the Igbo people's ultra-republicanism, and some go as far as blaming the current situation of Igbo political powerlessness in Nigeria on this resistance to recognizing a single leader. I think they are wrong. In a country mired in an unhealthy tradition of monarchy and centralization, I see the Igbo democratic disposition and equalitarian leadership as evidence of political development and refinement, one that should be emulated rather than derided.[3]

Biafra was not declared by the preferences of military leader Ojukwu alone. Instead, it was a product of a collegiate council comprised of

---

[1] The term 'Ndigbo' literally means 'Igbo people'. Now it is used in Nigerian politics to refer to the people of Igbo extraction, especially in reference to their collective political positions or platforms. Its current political usage was popularized by the pan-Igbo organization, Ohaneze Ndigbo (which literally translates as the rank and file).

[2] The Igbo State Union emerged out of the Igbo Union (later the Igbo Federal Union), formed in Lagos in 1936. It was a strong and enthusiastic partner of the Igbo-dominated nationalist political party, the National Council of Nigeria and the Cameroons (NCNC).

[3] The Igbo have been faithful to this model of politics for a long time. In part, it has accounted for their remarkable emphasis on individual achievement and initiative (Ottenberg 1962). I should also note that this type of political organization did not change even during the dire circumstances that led to the declaration of Biafra.

representatives from different provinces who took a decision to secede after General Yakubu Gowon backed out of the agreement reached in Aburi, Ghana. Even though Ojukwu was the military governor and a leading proponent of secession, he would never have been able to run Biafra alone. The point of this digression is to underscore the difficulty involved in leadership among Igbos to make us understand contextually Okigbo's leadership role after the war. When individualism is not checked by an equal dose of political common sense, when stubbornness and suicidal self-will replaces a quiet strategy and collective vision, a great nation such as the Igbo nation is bound to suffer great consequences.

THE END OF THE WAR

As I have said, the vindictive mentality of the Gowon regime after the war militated against the Igbo organizing effective political activity. After the war, Igbo leaders had to operate very carefully. When the ban on partisan politics was lifted in 1978, Ndigbo had neither the vision nor the leadership required to articulate a united Igbo platform for political competition at the national level. This was at the heart of the political problem faced by the Igbo then, and some say, even to this day. This lack of leadership was very visible in the Constituent Assembly of 1977, which was established to consider, amend and ratify the draft constitution that became the 1979 constitution. That assembly was, in fact, a platform for the formation and consolidation of political coalitions and alliances that were to shape the positions and policies of the political parties that competed for national power in the 1979 national election. Okigbo served as chairman of one of the committees of the Constitutional Drafting Committee as well as a member of the Constituent Assembly. According to Omo Omoruyi, an elected member of the Constituent Assembly, Okigbo deferred to the elected Igbo members, thus refusing to fill the vacuum of leadership among the Igbo members. As a result, unlike most of the other ethnoregional groups in the assembly, Ndigbo did not have a spokesperson to coordinate collective issue positions, although Alex Ekwueme, who became national vice-president in 1979, was expected to push for greater visibility of Ndigbo leaders.

This was why two Igbo non-members of the Constituent Assembly, Dr. Akanu Ibiam, former governor of the Eastern Region, and Dr. Nnamdi Azikiwe, (former governor-general, and later president of Nigeria), took over leadership by remotely controlling the elected Igbo members. Ibiam represented the anti-Sharia interest groups among the Igbo while Azikiwe represented the pro-North pressure elements. Okigbo, however, belonged to neither group. He saw the Igbo question in Nigerian politics very differently. He thought their immediate problem was not to capture the presidency but to erect a strong foundation composed of more states. This was because he saw states as the main bases for revenue sharing and the application of the principle of federal character. At this time in the nation's history, there were only two Igbo states (Imo and Anambra) as opposed to four Yoruba (Lagos, Ogun, Ondo and Oyo) and six Northern Nigerian states (Bauchi, Gongola, Kaduna, Kano, Niger and Sokoto). He believed that the Igbo needed to recapture their lost position of parity with the Yoruba and Hausa/Fulani ethnic majorities, and the only way to achieve this was through the creation of more Igbo states.[4] He recognized that after the civil war, states creation was no longer an issue for minority politics, but had become a major point of contestation in the political competition between the majority groups, with the Yoruba and the Hausa/Fulani each three states ahead of the Igbo.

Many Igbo leaders were particularly worried about the huge political and economic gap between Ndigbo and Yoruba. The legendary Igbo-Yoruba competition, (one reason for their relatively higher development levels vis-à-vis the North, and also for their political domination by the North) intensified after the 1930s when Nigerian nationalism began to be regionalized. Because this competition has been a constant theme in Nigerian politics, it is important to analyze it in some detail. The Yoruba saw the Igbo as more recent aspirants for prominent roles at the national level, and therefore a challenge to their own ascendancy. As noted by Okwudiba Nnoli, in the early 1940s the Yoruba were socioeconomically far ahead of the Igbo, whereas that socioeconomic gap was significantly narrowed between 1946 and 1964. This was precisely a period of high interethnic tension between the Igbo and Yoruba (Nnoli 1978, 224) Before the Igbo challenge, the Yoruba had dominated in the civil service, foreign private firms, education and Christian missionary activities, so they understandably resisted the rise of Igbo achievement. In response, Ndigbo saw their resistance as preserving Yoruba ascendancy.

---

[4] Before this time, the politics of state creation in Nigeria was championed by political parties dominated or founded by minority ethnic groups. Examples of such parties are the United Middle Belt Congress in the Jos plateau; the Bornu Youth Movement in the Northeast; the Ilorin Talaka Parapo in the North; the United Independent Party and the Niger Delta Congress in the Southeast; and the Benin-Delta Peoples, the Midwest State Movement and the Otu-Edo-NCNC in the Southwest. The agitation for states by minority groups in Nigeria has been attributed to the abnormal endowment of each of the three primary regions in Nigeria with a majority ethnic group and number of minority ethnic groups that occupy particular geographical areas. The push for separate states by these groups was necessitated by fears of discrimination, political and economic cultural marginalization by the majority groups. For a good historical discussion, see Osaghae 1998.

With regard to the political front, the Ndigbo position was as follows. First and foremost, Chief Obafemi Awolowo, the great Yoruba leader, failed to keep his promise that the West would secede from Nigeria if the East did so. This betrayal forced the Igbo to face the fury of Nigerian military might alone. Further, during the civil war, Awolowo, while serving in Gowon's government, initiated the policy of using hunger and starvation against Biafra. Moreover, Awolowo not only hastened to replace Igbo technocrats in the federal government with Yorubas during the war but also refused to reinstate the displaced Igbo after the war ended, greatly slowing down the reintegration of Ndigbo into the civil service and other areas of political life. Second, with regard to economic matters, Ndigbo resented several measures imposed by Awolowo that militated against a fast recovery of their devastated economy. At the end of the war, Awolowo 'decreed' that each Biafran who deposited any amount into his or her bank account during the war would receive compensation of only twenty Nigerian pounds, no matter how many millions of Biafran pounds he or she had on deposit. He also banned the importation of stockfish and secondhand clothes, speciality trades for many Igbo traders, thus compounding the sense of target exclusion. Lastly, immediately after the war, he pushed through the Indigenization Decree, fully aware that the majority of Ndigbo possessed only 20 Nigerian pounds (equivalent to US$30) to invest in private business. These moves ensured Yoruba domination of the Nigerian economy for some time to come.

Okigbo, however, and some other colleagues viewed Igbo-Yoruba competition differently. This group recognized that the traditional account described above did not adequately explain the influence of Moshood Abiola, a Yoruba who would carry the East in 1993. At the constitutional conference in 1979, Igbo-Yoruba rivalry was vitiated somewhat by the Igbo leaders like Okigbo and Ekwueme who saw the importance of a clear southern agenda for national restructuring. During the transition to civilian rule in the early 1990s, Babangida's imposition of a two party system — the National Republican Convention (NRC) and the Social Democratic Party (SDP) — showed the feasibility of a party arrangement that cuts across ethnic and regional rivalry. Later, after the death of General Sani Abacha in 1998, Ndigbo declared en masse for the People's Democratic Party (PDP), one of the new parties that arose to contest the elections in 2001. In particular, Ekwueme's support for the PDP drew in many Igbo leaders. He enjoyed much the same Ndigbo support in the 1980s and 1990s that Azikiwe had in the 1950s, an impressive show of unity. I believe that because of the pragmatism and foresight of Okigbo and other Igbo leaders of like mind, we are about to see the beginning of the end of that destructive rivalry between the two major southern ethnic groups.

For example, Okigbo was a passionate supporter of the June 12 movement for democracy. According to Omo Omoruyi (1999), President Babangida believed that the famous Okigbo Report, which forms the subject of Pita Agbese's chapter in this volume, was Okigbo's way of embarrassing the presidency because of his hostility to the June 12 annulment of the election results. 'I do not know your friend Pius is a NADECO[5] person', Babangida declared to Omoruyi. In fact, Babangida had anticipated that the findings of the Okigbo report would lend credibility to the military regime. Okigbo, however, has consistently defied such manipulation by any government.

Before the civil war, the Igbo-Yoruba rivalry had reached a sort of equilibrium; however, by its conclusion, the Yoruba were far ahead of the Igbo in both socioeconomic and political power. To regain political significance at the national level, Ndigbo had to re-establish parity with the Yoruba in the south and to regain its voice in national affairs. Ndigbo leaders set goals to secure more proportionate appointments of Ndigbo to high government and military positions and to make the Ndigbo voice heard. To achieve these goals, Ndigbo needed more states and their own newspapers.

Okigbo took part in the planning to start a national Ndigbo newspaper that would articulate Igbo policy positions and promote Igbo candidates for political office. Imo State University sent personnel to help in this effort. Although, these plans did not materialize at this time, two participants in the original plan went on to establish newspapers of their own: Chief Emmanuel Iwuanyanwu founded *The Champion* and Sunny Odogwu set up *The Post Express*, both based in Lagos. The most important instrument for the articulation of Ndigbo's collective political strategy and policy positions, however, was an organization that authoritatively spoke for them. This need gave rise to the formation of the pan-Igbo organization, Ohaneze Ndigbo.

OHANEZE NDIGBO

Ohaneze Ndigbo is an amorphous alliance, encompassing a wide array of Igbo sociocultural associations and leadership, seeking to expand Igbo participation in national life. Its members are free to follow any political affiliation of their choice, so there is very little in the way of 'party discipline'. Instead stiff competition exists among both its membership and

---

[5] NADECO stands for National Democratic Coalition formed in 1994 as one of the grouping of civil rights and democracy activists that fought against the annulment of June 12.

leadership in national politics.[6] Although some professional members of Ndigbo community see Ohaneze Ndigbo as too obtuse and amorphous to effectively champion the Igbo cause, it has quietly influenced the discourse on the future direction of Nigerian politics. The current de facto recognition of the six geopolitical zones in Nigeria and the constant clamour for the rotation of the presidency testify to the effectiveness of the alliance.

Okigbo played a significant role in the formation of Ohaneze Ndigbo and served as its secretary. Indeed, most of the initial meetings took place in his home. Even before Ohaneze Ndigbo was formed, many viewed him as a possible political leader of Ndigbo.[7] In fact, some Igbo leaders had actually urged him to stand as a presidential candidate at one time. But the truth is that Okigbo could never have been a successful Igbo politician. He was loyal to his people. Although he could easily have left Biafra during the civil war, he chose to stay and serve the secessionist government for which he was subsequently imprisoned by the federal government. Very aristocratic in bearing, he was inclined to keep his own council, a deportment that does not necessarily go down well with Igbos. He never saw himself as part of the crowd. This particular disposition defined and limited his role in Ohaneze Ndigbo. He loved to think things through. He had the ability to organize ideas to rally people and to present ideas effectively for general deliberation. Yet he had little patience for the 'palaver' favoured by Ndigbo. In this respect, he stood out from the general membership of the Ohaneze. Despite his importance, he was never fond of joining delegations to Aso Rock in Abuja. Instead, he worked very hard behind the scenes with Ekwueme and other colleagues to advance the Igbo position through those dark days of the Abacha regime.

On the whole, he can be truthfully defined as an intellectual leader for Ndigbo, one who carried himself with great dignity but who lacked the charisma and popularity to carry this quality over to political leadership. He enjoyed great respect because of his intellect and integrity. Perhaps one of the greatest values of Okigbo to Ndigbo was his great ability to tell people off. In certain ways, Okigbo was not partisan. He could criticize anyone and still get his views seriously considered. Many Igbo leaders therefore used him to rope in recalcitrant Igbos and put them in their place. As the chairman

---

[6] For example, in the last national election Ekwueme opposed Olusegun Obasanjo for the PDP nomination, but Ohaneze Ndigbo failed to persuade Jim Nwobodo to support Ekwueme even though the two politicians are both major power brokers in the organization.

[7] However, Dr. Sylvester Ugoh assures me that Okigbo was at the end of the war not seeking to be the political leader of the Igbos. For one thing, Igbo leaders were targets for imprisonment (telephone conversation, May 25, 2001).

of SKOUP and Co., a successful international consulting firm that undertook projects for the Organization of African Unity, the United Nations and other international agencies, he was a man of means. Yet, it is not clear if he ever funded projects for Ohaneze Ndigbo. It appears that while he could make personal sacrifices for Ndigbo, he remained a great pragmatist throughout his life.

He has been described variously as tireless, efficient, sharp and possessing a very wide knowledge base. He was also cosmopolitan, and very comfortable with both Nigerians and foreigners. He was a man of the world, a committed Biafran and a comfortable Nigerian. His legacy is as important as that of General Aguiyi Ironsi, with whom he shared the ideal of 'one Nigeria'. In fact, Okigbo was probably the last pan-Nigerian intellectual of Igbo extraction. His death marks the end of a truly Nigerian person.

REFERENCES

Nnoli, Okwudiba. 1978. *Ethnic Politics in Nigeria.* Enugu, Nigeria: Fourth Dimensions.

Omoruyi, Omo. 1999. *The Tale of June 12: The Betrayal of the Democratic Rights of Nigerians (1993).* London: Press Alliance Network Limited.

Osaghae, Eghosa E. 1998. *Crippled Giant: Nigeria since Independence.* London: Hurst and Company.

Ottenberg, Simon. 1962. 'Ibo Receptivity to Changes'. In W. Bascom and M. J. Herskovits (eds.), *Continuity and Change in African Cultures,* 130–143. Chicago: University of Chicago Press.

PART III: ECONOMIC POLICY AND PUBLIC FINANCE IN NIGERIA AND AFRICA

7

OKIGBO'S LEGACY AND CONTRIBUTIONS IN AFRICAN ECONOMICS, PUBLIC POLICY AND FINANCE

Emmanuel Nnadozie

INTRODUCTION

Why has sustainable economic development eluded African countries despite the wisdom, important contributions and informed advisement of such economic development experts as Pius Okigbo? Sustainable economic development has eluded African countries not because of bad advice from such highly esteemed experts as Okigbo, but because African governments have ignored the sound advice of these experts.

An economist and scholar who served the British colonial, the contemporary Nigerian and other independent African governments, Okigbo was one of Africa's foremost intellectuals. During his illustrious career, he served in many capacities at both the continental and national levels. Among other accomplishments, he was the first Nigerian economic adviser to the Eastern Nigerian Government, the first economic adviser to the federal government of Nigeria and the first Nigerian ambassador to the European Economic Community (EEC). As the Nigerian ambassador to the EEC, headquartered in Brussels, he participated in the subsequent agreement between the African, Caribbean and Pacific Group of States (ACP) and the European group. In addition, he was at the centre of economic planning in Nigeria, particularly in public finance, where he worked on the preparation of most of the federal national development plans (NDP) and Eastern Region development plans. He is probably best remembered as the chairman of the 1976 panel for a review of Nigeria's financial system, the most elaborate work done in that area to date.

Okigbo was a prodigious scholar and a well-rounded economist as evidenced by his publications. He was an expert in public finance, banking and financial economics who exerted significant influence on fiscal policy in Nigeria. His legacy derives not only from his public service performance and contributions in governance and administration, but also from his scholarly and intellectual contributions. For an intellectual who was not permanently in academia, his work filled important voids and provided vital information and knowledge. This chapter focuses on Okigbo's contributions and legacy in the scholarship of Nigerian and African economic policy and public finance. It examines Okigbo's major economic works comparatively and thematically. In identifying and comparing the central themes and approaches, it asks the central question: What are Okigbo's fundamental ideas and impact on economics and finance? How did he influence our understanding of African economic policy, public finance and financial systems? In what ways did Okigbo present his economic thoughts and how are they relevant? This chapter also considers the relevance of Okigbo's writing to contemporary African development challenges.

OKIGBO'S OVERALL CONTRIBUTIONS
Okigbo was a heterodox economist who employed the Marxian historical and Schumpeterian methods. Above all, he was eclectic and pragmatic – a practical economist – in the Ricardian and Marshallian tradition. Yet, by no means does this imply that Okigbo was not an original thinker without an original methodology. He understood that economics exists for humans, not humans for economics. It was said that Marx read everything before he wrote anything; Okigbo read everything and wrote everything. He understood the importance of capital – financial, physical and human – in the growth and development equation. In his work, he developed policy-oriented ideas and problem-solving options on the following issues:

- the need to recognize the uniqueness of African economics, which needed to be looked at within historical, social, political and philosophical frameworks;
- the need to have a holistic approach in the analysis of economic problems and to tap into one's own experience in the real world;
- the centrality of capital (physical, financial and human) in the African development equation;
- the appropriate role of the state and planning in the development process;
- the appropriate development strategies, much of which are today being promoted by the World Bank and the International Monetary

Fund, in terms of deregulation, decentralization, fiscal discipline and monetary controls;
- the appropriate place and role of monetarism and financial systems in an African economic system;
- the need for a strong and autonomous central bank;
- the importance of economic and regional cooperation for African development;
- the problem of Africa's debt burden and its profound economic consequences.

Moreover, Okigbo enlightens us on many other economic and policy-related issues, including the internal and external sources and conditions of growth, the importance of matching economic efficiency goals with those of equity and freedom, and the similarity of the productive sectors of African countries.

One can see in Okigbo's work and everyday activities Marshallian humanism mixed with a healthy dose of utilitarianism as well as the nationalism of his contemporaries Nnamdi Azikiwe (first Nigerian governor-general and then first president of Nigeria from 1963–1966) and Michael Okpara (Eastern Region premier from 1960 to 1966). Like the latter politicians, Okigbo had no difficulty in being an Igbo and a Nigerian at the same time. He transcended the imperatives and demands of his community and Igbo interests to perform a significant role as a nationalist and a Pan-Africanist.

CONTRIBUTION TO AFRICAN ECONOMICS AND DEVELOPMENT

The publication that aptly captures Okigbo's philosophy of economics is *Economic Growth, Development and Freedom* (c.1982). In this work, he discusses his views about the right path to development, how to mobilize resources for the successful implementation of projects and the role that freedom plays in the whole process. He believes that institutions matter and that there is a need to reconcile economic efficiency with equity. He also addresses the issue of appropriate rewards through allocative and distributive efficiency. Acutely aware of the problems involved in determining the gross domestic product (GDP) and growth rate without adequate statistics, he reflects on Nigeria's dilemma of planning without data. Okigbo warns against over-reliance on available numbers to tell us more than they can, examining the stark distinction between growth and development.

AFRICAN REGIONALISM AND INTERNATIONAL ECONOMICS

Okigbo's contribution to the dialogue on African regionalism and the international dimension of African economics began with one of his earliest publications, *Africa and the Common Market* (1967). In this study, he draws on his personal knowledge and experience as Nigeria's first ambassador to the EEC, detailing the evolution of his country's negotiations with that body for the benefit of policy-makers and others interested in international economic relations (p. viii).

The book provides the reader with a comprehensive, well-researched review of the genesis, evolution and transformation of the EEC. It provides vital background information on the EEC and its affiliate, the Association of African Countries (AAC). After describing the formation and dynamics of the EEC, the study details the history of regionalism and economic co-operation in Africa. Indeed, this treatise provides invaluable insight into the functioning of regionalism, the competition between Nigeria and the AAC, the various agreements among African states, those between Europe and Africa, and the complexities introduced by Britain and the Commonwealth that threatened the very existence of the EEC. It remains the seminal work on this subject and laid the foundation for subsequent scholarship on regionalism in Africa.

In *Africa and the Common Market*, Okigbo raises several critical questions. He begins with a discourse on the dynamics surrounding the origins of African regional and continental integration and the relations of African countries with the EEC. He then dissects Africa's unequal relationship with the EEC, showing that this relationship was neither accidental nor fortuitous. The seeds of European postcolonial exploitative tendencies were sown from the inception of EEC. Indeed, Article 131 of the Treaty of Rome, which provides for the formation of the association of the former colonies, explicitly defines the nature of the EEC's relationship to the former colonies (or associated members as they were called). The colonies concerned were those of Belgium, France, Italy and the Netherlands, the majority of which were in Africa.

According to Okigbo, the participation of these non-European, quasi members in the EEC alliance was not necessarily by choice. He opines that as the community evolved from a customs union into an economic union, its members (Germany, France, Italy, the Netherlands, Belgium and Luxembourg) benefited greatly from a variety of preferential arrangements. In contrast, non-European associated members (most were in Africa) benefited only from reciprocal tariff reductions. Likewise, he pointedly demonstrates that the associated states were required to specialize in agricultural goods while the European members specialized in industrial manufactured goods, which the former was expected to import: in short, a blatant repetition of their former colonial relationship. In reality, he contends, the associated members were never integrated among themselves or with the EEC. Instead, they served as captive African markets for the EEC.

By writing about regional and international integration when he did, Okigbo was a visionary whose pioneering work provided the basic foundation and building blocks for much of modern African economics. Partly because of his work, many African scholars and policy-makers were persuaded that some form of regional collaboration, cooperation, or coordination is inevitable for self-sustaining development. The process of African industrialization requires regional cooperation. Such cooperation will enhance the free flow of people, capital and technology across the nations involved; create trade and enhance incomes and welfare; improve information, labour and capital flows for increased investment; and encourage technology transfer. Moreover, regional cooperation should foster political stability through induced democratic reforms and mutual political reinforcement by regional political organizations.

DEVELOPMENT PLANNING

Okigbo's contribution to African economics does not end with his writing on regionalism. In his book, *National Development Planning in Nigeria 1900–92* (1989), he deals with the evolution, transformation and critique of economic planning for development purposes in Nigeria. This important work focuses on two things: the evolution of centralized planning in economic development and the issue of fiscal federalism. It examines key periods in planning, highlighting phases of rupture and transformation. His analysis rests on classical economic theory, mostly Adam Smith's thought on the 'duties of the sovereign', which is '...the provision of internal justice; protection from external aggression; and undertaking of social works' – to delineate the role of the public sector and advocate its intervention in the economic system (p.6). Okigbo explains that Nigeria's import substitution policy, which has been blamed for the failure of sustainable growth in the country, began during the colonial period with the first ten-year development plan (1946–1955). 'It was recognized', he states, 'that Nigeria should face more towards the internal market than the export market...' (p. 20).

Okigbo divides the history of economic planning in Nigeria into two chronological phases: the first period spanning the years 1900–1945, and the second beginning in 1946 and continuing after independence. The origins of contemporary economic planning in Nigeria began in the second period, manifested in the First Ten-Year Plan of Development and Welfare for Nigeria (1946–1955). Concerning this plan, Okigbo (1989b, 32) contends:

The real criticism of the Ten-Year Plan is not that there were no overall macro-economic targets to use as reference; rather, it is that there was no set of explicit statements as to how the goals proposed in the Plan should be achieved. The Plan document did not indicate what policies should be used to ensure that the proposals were fully carried out, that the local Nigerian revenues would be raised to meet local financial commitments, and that foreign loans would be serviced.

Nigeria's experience with modern planning developed through five national development plans: 1962–1968, 1970–1974, 1975–1980, 1981–1985 and 1988–1992. For comparative purposes, Okigbo surveys similar plans in the Gold Coast and French West Africa and the ideas embodied in them. None of them achieved their full objectives, he declared. In Nigeria, the factors that contributed to the failure of planning included problems involved in the process of concentration and centralization, the use of an inappropriate model and lack of discipline in executing the plan. Interestingly, Okigbo concluded that the main problem in planning resulted from the emphasis on centralization and concentration. 'Far too much of the planning function', he maintained, 'is concentrated in the Ministry of National Planning; a role that it is hardly equipped to fulfil either from the point of view of prestige and influence or from that of technical competence' (p.161). He stops short of advocating an abrogation of development planning in Nigeria but identifies such problems as inadequate methodology, wrong theoretical foundation and the lack of follow-up. From this book, we note that Okigbo was well aware of the debate between laissez-faire and planning as well as the various models of planning then in existence.

CONTRIBUTION TO PUBLIC FINANCE IN NIGERIA

In the economic history of contemporary Nigeria, fiscal federalism and revenue allocation have proved to be constant sources of tension and conflict due to their inherent unfairness and politicization. Oil has taken centre stage as the main determinant of the politics and patterns of revenue allocation. With oil dominance came federal government control of national revenue and a progressive neglect of the regions from which oil revenues emerge (Nnadozie 1995, 2000; Nwuke 2001). But even before the emergence of an oil-centred and rancorous system of fiscal federalism, Okigbo had provided Nigeria with invaluable insight into its experience in public finance.

In *Nigerian Public Finance* (1955), Okigbo analyzes the country's history, structure and patterns of federal, regional and local government finance. This work, drafted while he served on a British government fiscal commission in Kenya, marked the first attempt to synthesize and systematically explore the evolution of Nigeria's fiscal system and relationships. He laments the low level of government allocations to productive sectors such as agriculture and warns that a heavy tax burden will result in a negative impact on economic growth. Ironically, the remedies he suggests are much the same as those now promoted by the International Monetary Fund as a solution to the economic ills of many African countries, including Nigeria. Had Nigeria heeded his warnings, perhaps the country might not have suffered the severe economic woes it experienced in the 1990s and continues to suffer.

Okigbo's investigation shows the importance of public policy in economic development and government accountability. His assessment helps us understand why so many Nigerians are presently disenchanted with, even distrustful of, the government. One reason is the government's total failure to develop public policy in Nigeria, exemplified by its apparent inability to use its oil wealth to resolve socioeconomic problems. He maintains that in a free market the government may wield its economic functions to free society from ignorance, unemployment, poverty, disease, crime, discrimination and other ills. The output of goods and services, employment, income and prices are determined by a variety of policies and regulations, including antitrust laws, labour laws and fiscal and monetary policy. These policies affect tax levels, consumption, investment, money supply, interest rates and trade. Good governance, however, has been seriously lacking in the country. This will continue until an appropriate constitutional framework for reform can be created.

According to Okigbo, 'The evolution of the current pattern of fiscal structure and relationships in Nigeria is a reflection of its constitutional history' (p. 4). This statement, written in 1955, could easily have been written in 2001, for Nigeria still contends with the same issue that Okigbo highlighted 36 years previously: the centrality of the constitution in national economic development. Now Nigerians realize how much the constitution affects resource and asset allocation and income distribution. Okigbo traces this back to the Native Authority Act of 1904 and 1906, which defined the tax collection system and revenue sharing formula between the British administration and the native authorities. Thus, he argues, the amalgamation of Northern and Southern Nigeria in 1914 represents 'the first major landmark in the evolution of Nigerian fiscal relationships' (p.7). The amalgamation itself was financially motivated to reduce the dependency of the North on Britain by supporting it with revenue from the more financially viable South. Efforts to reorient the financial system began after World War II and ever since then economic planners have tried to balance derivation and need in determining a revenue allocation formula between the Nigerian federal government and the regions, and later the states.

A second work, *Nigeria's Financial System* (1981), underscores Okigbo's contribution to theories and practices of banking, financial economics and public finance. Before this study, literature on Nigeria's financial system was practically nonexistent. His book is the watershed publication on Nigeria's financial system. In fact, an entire era in the history of banking in Nigeria is often referred to as the post-Okigbo era (Nunnally, Plath and Nnadozie, 2000). This nomenclature itself testifies to his influence in financial theory in Nigeria.

Nwankwo (1990) reports that present-day banking in Nigeria has two objectives: (1) to standardize and increase the proportion of Nigerian ownership in the domestic banking industry, and (2) to facilitate and help sustain rural economic development. In 1976, Okigbo was appointed chairman of a committee mandated to appraise Nigeria's system of finance and recommend reforms. The committee's report formed the basis of a government white paper published in March 1977 (Okigbo 1981, 23–25). The Okigbo white paper recommended that the federal government revise the objectives of the country's financial system and its major component, the banking system, to facilitate the effective management of the economy, to provide noninflationary support for the economy, to achieve greater mobilization of savings and to ensure efficient transfer of domestic deposits between lenders and borrowers. The role of the banking system, he insisted, should facilitate the transformation of the rural environment by promoting the rapid expansion of banking facilities and services. The establishment of rural banks would promote banking habits among rural dwellers by creating paying and receiving stations for hand-to-hand currency exchange. Moreover, by providing payment facilities for the transfer of funds between rural and urban areas, they would serve as a vehicle for the mobilization of savings and creation of credit facilities to fund economic development in rural areas (Nwankwo 1991, 23–25).

Another area that interested Okigbo was the role of a central bank in national economic policy. It is well known that in the United States the constitution provides for congressional action to establish monetary authorities and control systems to ensure the smooth running of the economy. Consequently, the independence of the U.S. Federal Reserve prevents the politicization of monetary policy and makes it possible for the independent Federal Reserve to act in the interest of the economy. Although Nigeria has often found inspiration in United States institutions, it did not incorporate the idea of an independent central bank in any of its early constitutions. In

1981, Okigbo warned against the legal limitations imposed on the Central Bank of Nigeria (CBN):

> In our view, the law needs to be changed: even if the law is retained as it is, the exercise of the powers conferred on the Minister of Finance requires caution. It requires, more importantly, an appreciation that the Central Bank is not a department of the ministry and that the Governor of Central Bank and the Board of Directors have a primary responsibility to the nation and should, therefore, be directly accountable for the success or failure of the monetary policy (Okigbo, 1981, p. 274).

Once again, Okigbo was on target in anticipating the problems resulting from the existence of a politically vulnerable central bank. Had his warning been heeded, Nigeria may have been able to head off the major financial crises of the late 1980s and 1990s and perhaps averted the bank failures of the late 1990s. Saddled with political manipulation and control, the CBN was unable to exercise its supervisory role during the extraordinary banking boom.

In a lecture entitled, *Reforming the Nigerian Banking System in the 1990's*, delivered at the Nigerian Institute of Bankers in Lagos, Okigbo addresses the issue of bank reform. After evaluating the existing Banking Decree of 1969, the Central Bank Act and the Companies Act, he emphasized that the role of the banking system was to establish a system of deposit and payments, finance and credit, and money creation. An adequate banking system, he contended, sets up facilities within easy reach of the customers. They should not have to travel great distances to a bank, wait in long queues for service, or curry favour with the clerk. In his view, Nigeria is under-banked in terms of bank-population ratio and in terms of the proportion of transactions. He urged an overhaul of the banking industry through the introduction of modern sophisticated and specialized banking tools, increased rural banking and strengthening of banking regulation. Throughout, his focus was on the importance of an efficient system accessible by the entire population.

OTHER CONTRIBUTIONS TO ECONOMICS

Through his other publications – *Essays in the Public Philosophy of Development* (1987–1993), *Towards a Reconstruction of the Political Economy of Igbo Civilization* (1986), *Okparanomics: the Economic and Social Philosophy of Michael Okpara* (1987) and *The African Debt Trap* (1989a) – Okigbo continued his examination of the political economy of development. These represented an eclectic mix of essays, speeches and a monograph that ranged over various aspects of the economic crisis that followed the collapse of the oil boom, subsequent devaluation of the naira and the structural adjustment program. As an Igbo himself, he felt that it was important to understand the dynamics and history of the indigenous Igbo economic system and how it fared in the wider Nigerian economy. Igbo politicians and public figures from Nnamdi Azikiwe (first indigenous governor-general of Nigeria and then the country's first president)) and Michael Okpara (premier of the Eastern Region, 1960–1966) to the present elected governors of Imo and Anambra states have had successful careers as entrepreneurs and, hence, tended to support private enterprise. Forrest (1994, 250) observes, 'It is not a coincidence that these communities have been in the vanguard of recent efforts to industrialize'. In his 1986 Ahiajoku lecture: 'Towards a Reconstruction of the Political Economy of Igbo Civilization' Okigbo concluded that:

> The Igbos had demonstrated that with the appropriate support and under suitable environment, a totally indigenous technological civilization was possible in black Africa. Many of us had hoped, after the war, that Nigeria, now aware of what is possible, would seek to reenact that achievement by simulating and creating those conditions that could best promote it. But with the end of the war, the Nigerian authorities dismantled and demobilized both the spirit and the effort. There is, I believe, ample room for the Igbo to bring to bear on the solution of Nigerian economic and political problems some unique contribution.

Okigbo's ideas developed and transformed over time and occasionally raised controversy. A careful look at his works shows the temporal and idiosyncratic dynamism of his thought. This is best illustrated by his position on the role of central planning in the economic system of developing countries and the issue of fiscal federalism. In his early writings on central planning, he strongly supported development planning as a means of achieving rapid economic progress despite its limitations. After all, he started his public service career as a development officer. In the later stages of his career, however, he became a strong critic of development planning, at least as it operated in Nigeria and elsewhere in Africa. By the 1980s and 1990s, his writings show that his view of the role of the state had significantly shifted in favour of the market, be it in the domestic economic arena or in the international domain. In his essay on the challenges of the programs created by international financial institutions for sub-Saharan Africa, he opines that globalization was neither fortuitous nor inevitably perilous and advises that African countries strategically integrate themselves into the global economic system.

In the area of fiscal federalism – an area of great contention and controversy – Okigbo seriously revised his initial advocacy for the highly polemical derivation-based allocation formula. As chair of the revenue allocation commission in 1979, he argued against the principle of derivation, and recommended instead a revenue allocation formula that invested the greater share of revenue in the Nigerian federal government. Clearly, the macroeconomic impact of this formula was significant. 'Over the years, Nigeria's fiscal federalism model has resulted in a situation, whereby the oil-producing states received less revenue than the non-oil producing states' (Nnadozie, 2002, 25). Thus, oil will remain a source of economic distortion, rent-seeking and conflict as long as the federal government insists on employing its present policy. So far, its track record in managing oil revenues has been very poor.

CONCLUSION

Okigbo made a significant contribution to the understanding of African economics and finance, especially through his focus on the Nigerian economy. Although his writings centred mainly on the Nigerian economy, he also wrote on politics and governance. Notwithstanding his financial and economic focus, his eclecticism and polyvalent scholarship underscore his immense contribution to Africa. These attributes make Okigbo's writings invaluable tools of policy-making, education and intellectual discourse. An overview of his publications shows that he systematically started with financial analysis, moved on to the political economy and development philosophy and ended with development planning. By concentrating on the centrality of private and public finance in the economic system in his early writings, he established the groundwork for his later emphasis on the philosophy and political economy of development.

Okigbo used a historical approach in analyses that evaluated the origin, evolution and transformation of major economic and financial institutions and policies. Deeply aware of the temporal and circumstantial issues surrounding his writing and his position as a pioneer, he delivers, in each instance, a masterful exposé on the major periods or phases and identifies the critical junctures and major ruptures in occurrence. Therein lies the key contribution he made to African economics and finance, for he made it possible for subsequent scholars to build upon his magna opus and expatiate on these subjects. On the whole, he was able to show a great deal of dynamism and pragmatism in terms of the prevailing economic paradigm and ideology of the time.

REFERENCES

Forrest, Tom. 1994. *The Advance of African Capital: The Growth of Nigerian Private Enterprise*. London: Edinburgh University Press.

Nnadozie, E. 1995. *Oil and Socioeconomic Crisis in Nigeria: A Regional Perspective to the Nigerian Disease and the Rural Sector.* Lewiston: Mellen University Press.

_____. 2000. 'The Constitution and Economic Development in Nigeria'. Paper presented at the conference on 'Nigerian Diaspora and 1999 Constitution. Colin Powell Center, City University of New York, New York, March 23–24.

_____. 2002. 'Are Growth and Development Constitutional Issues in Nigeria?' Paper presented at the Centre for the Study of African Economies, Oxford University sixth annual conference 'Understanding Poverty and Growth in Sub-Saharan Africa', St Catherine's College, Oxford, March 18–19, 2002.

Nwankwo, G.O. 1990. *Prudential Regulation of Nigerian Banking*. Lagos: University of Lagos Press.

Nunnally, Bennie H, Jr., D. Anthony Plath and Emmanuel Nnadozie. 2000. 'Contemporary Banking and Bank Regulation in Nigeria'. *The Journal of International Banking Regulation* 2(2):51–60.

Nwuke, Kasirim O. 2001. 'Managing Multi-Ethnicity: Lessons from Nigeria'. Paper presented at the Institute on Race and Social Division, Boston University, January 3.

Okigbo, P.N.C. 1955. *Nigerian Public Finance*. African Studies series, No. 15. Evanston, IL: Northwestern University Press.

_____. 1962. *Nigerian National Accounts, 1950–1957*. Lagos: Federal Ministry of Economic Development.

_____. 1967. *Africa and the Common Market*. Evanston: Northwestern University Press.

_____. 1981. *Nigeria's Financial System*. London: Longman.

_____. c.1982. *Economic Growth, Development and Freedom*. University lecture delivered on the occasion of the third convocation on Friday, December 18, 1981. Maiduguri: Borno State: University of Maiduguri.

_____. Between 1983 and 1988. *Reforming the Nigerian Banking System in the 1990's*. Lecture delivered to the Nigerian Institute of Bankers. Lagos: Nigerian Institute of Bankers.

_____. 1986. *Towards a Reconstruction of the Political Economy of Igbo Civilization*. Owerri, Imo State [Nigeria]: Ministry of Information, Culture, Youth and Sports.

_____. 1987. *Okparanomics: The Economic and Social Philosophy of Michael Okpara*. S.l.: s.n.

_____. 1987–1993. *Essays in the Public Philosophy of Development*. 4v. Enugu: Fourth Dimension Publishing. Company.

_____. 1989a. *The African Debt Trap*. Lagos: University of Lagos Press.

_____. 1989b. *National Development Planning in Nigeria 1900–92*. London: James Currey.

_____. 1999. 'Le projet de mondialisation et de dévelopement des organismes financiers internationaux, un défi pour l'Afrique subsaharienne'. In *Les Organismes financiers internationaux, instruments de l'économie politique libérale*, 100–120. Paris: L'Harmattan for Centre Tricontinental Louvain-la-Neuve.

\

8

THE STATE-BUSINESS NEXUS IN NIGERIA: THE ROLE OF INDIGENOUS CONSULTANTS

Clement E. Adibe

INTRODUCTION

Pius Okigbo is hardly a household name in Nigeria. Much of his enormous intellectual achievements took place outside the glare of the media. For the most part, his works are accessible mainly to scholars, especially those with an abiding interest in development economics or, as political scientists prefer to call it, comparative development. Unlike his fellow kinsman, Chief Jerome Udoji, whose postcivil war commission recommended the retroactive increase in the wages of public servants in 1974, Okigbo's activities as a leading consultant to Nigeria's federal government's development plans did not have such a visible and immediate an impact on the people (Udoji 1974).[1] Yet, while Udoji's salaries have long disappeared, Okigbo's influence on development theory in Nigeria remains deep and will continue to shape public policy for a long time to come. My objective in this chapter is to examine the implications on the complex state-business nexus in Nigeria of Okigbo's activities as one of the earliest indigenous consultants to the federal government on matters of economic development. To this end, I pose three basic questions to which there are no easy answers:

1. What is the impact of Okigbo's thought on the complex relationship between the state and private capital in Nigeria?

---

[1] In his Preface to *National Development Planning in Nigeria, 1900–92*, Okigbo (1989, ix) acknowledges his role 'as a member, or as the chairman of, several government commissions appointed to study various branches of [development] activity in Nigeria'.

2. What philosophy informed Okigbo's thought on Nigeria's economic development and what is its relevance to Nigeria's contemporary economic problems?

3. How did Okigbo escape the problems of sycophancy and corruption that are so pervasive among those who walk Nigeria's corridors of power?

PIUS OKIGBO AND *DIRIGISME*

Much of Okigbo's writings can be read as a sustained attempt to adapt systematically the theoretical insights of development economics to the peculiarities of his country Nigeria.[2] He was a product of his time, a time when academic thinking on comparative development was shaped by the ubiquitous ideological push and pull of the Cold War era. It is to Okigbo's credit that he sought to breathe some pragmatism into the application of competing theories of development by identifying aspects of neoliberalism and *dirigisme* to accommodate the sociohistorical contexts of Nigeria. Thus, in *National Development Planning in Nigeria* (1989), Okigbo meticulously draws upon the works of Adam Smith, the father of neoliberal economics, on which to build an elaborate economic model. 'In the eighteenth century', Okigbo writes:

> Adam Smith defined the duties of the 'sovereign' as provision of internal justice; protection from external aggression; and the undertaking of social works. According to this approach, then, the state has the duty to create those conditions of orderly living in which each citizen can carry out his or her daily activities *such as are permitted by the prevailing rules and regulations* [emphasis added]. (Okigbo 1989, 6).

Not unlike Marx, Okigbo's acknowledgement of Smith does not render him neo-Smithian by any means and the caveat he inserts at the end of his paraphrase of Smith ensures that the economic theory he intends to develop for his country is nuanced enough to recognize the fallacy of Smith's limited government. His target, of course, is the 'duty' of the state to undertake social works.

> Smith's third class of duties of a sovereign can be broken down into further sub-classes: allocation and use of resources (covering the efficient

---

[2] Amongst Okigbo's published works, the following stand out in terms of their influence on development theory and public policy: 'Criteria for Public Expenditures on Education' (1964); *Nigerian Public Finance* (1965); *Africa and the Common Market* (1967); *Nigeria's Financial System* (1981); and *National Development Planning in Nigeria, 1900–92* (1989).

use of resources); distribution (covering 'equitable' distribution of income and wealth) and stability (covering employment and stable prices). It is presumed that the success of the state in promoting these objectives is built around the welfare of the citizen (Okigbo 1989, 7).

Absent from this analysis is any discussion by Okigbo of Smith's caveat that the state's involvement in the economic sphere be limited only to those crucial areas that private capital is unable or unwilling to undertake. The reason for this omission, of course, is Okigbo's bias in favour of some form of centralized planning under the auspices of the state:

> Our view of the needs of future planning is that we should borrow a leaf from the Mahalanobis model for India, link it with the Kornai concept of planning and marry both with the experience of the French indicative planning scheme (Okigbo 1989, 201).

It is to this particular goal that Okigbo devotes much of his intellectual energy, recognizing as he did that such a scheme:

> ...would have to be supplemented with a deeper consultation of and participation by, the private sector along the lines of the indicative planning procedure. It would need to be supported by a multitude of special studies and investigations and by investment of considerable resources in research and development and in the collection, processing and storage of data (Okigbo 1989, 203).

We may therefore view some of Okigbo's statistical studies, such as *Nigerian National Accounts* (1962) and *Nigeria's Financial System* (1981) as his response to the challenges posed by Stolper's *Planning without Facts* (1966). In that case, it is apropos to recall Stolper's cautionary words:

> The 'lack of facts' to which this book refers cannot be remedied by organizing the collection of more and better statistics. *The basic problem is that all too often it is quite unclear precisely what question should be asked; sometimes the question is asked wrongly; and it is by no means certain that answers always exist* [author's italics] (p.7).

In the context of the sifting sand that is the Nigerian State, one can only wish that Okigbo had heeded this advice and had exercised greater caution in expressing his faith in *dirigisme*. It should by now be obvious that state planning in Nigeria, which he so strongly promoted and supported, has been an unmitigated failure. As Julius Ihonvbere (1994, 16) unambiguously put it:

> One does not require a degree in economics to know that the Nigerian economy and society, in spite of vitriolic and suffocating propaganda by the state and its agents, has not succeeded since the 1970s in meeting any of the objectives [of the development plans]. The reasons for this are of course embedded in (a) the character of planning; (b) the content and context of planning, in particular, the ideology of plan initiation and implementation; (c) the role of the state in the planning process; (d) the use to which planning has been put by the dominant classes since political independence.

Furthermore, Ihonvbere continues, 'A state-directed development planning in Nigeria has tended to widen the gap between the rich and the poor, promote alienation and tensions, [and] increase the marginalization of the majority from the planning processes' (p.16).

These weaknesses of centralized planning, some of which Okigbo had acknowledged in his studies, raise a very interesting question. Why did Okigbo continue to support state-directed national development plans despite its manifest weaknesses and failure? Could Okigbo's trust in the developmentalist capacity of the Nigerian state have been misplaced and naïve? Was he, like so many of us, fooled by our abiding optimism in the ability of the Nigerian state to 'do the right thing', despite mounting evidence to the contrary? As we now know from the World Bank's manifest frustrations and sometimes outright failure in pushing Nigeria along the path of free market economics, even Smith would not have fared better. The reason, in my view, is rather simple. The phenomenon of underdevelopment, to which much economic theorizing is devoted, is a political rather than an economic problem in many developing countries, especially Nigeria. To rephrase Clinton's 1992 campaign slogan: 'It's the politics, stupid!' As Amartya Sen (2000, 3) has argued recently, development is the 'process of expanding the real freedoms that people enjoy'. It involves the 'removal of major sources of unfreedom: poverty as well as tyranny, poor economic opportunities as well as systematic social deprivation, neglect of public facilities as well as intolerance or overactivity of repressive states'. Put simply, underdevelopment is a political asset in the hands of despots who desire nothing more than the continual servitude of their own people. I shall return to this issue later in the essay, but in the meantime, it would be useful to examine the theoretical currents that underpinned Okigbo's *dirigisme*, for he was not alone in prescribing a heavy state presence in Africa's economy if only to enhance the presence of indigenous capital.

COMPARATIVE DEVELOPMENT THEORIES AND
THE SIGNIFICANCE OF INDIGENOUS CAPITAL

The state-business nexus remains one of the most compelling areas of inquiry in political economy. For a political scientist, especially a student of conflict resolution, this relationship is particularly fascinating because it is inherently ill-defined and susceptible to the temporal variations in culture, politics, norms and even personalities. It is, therefore, a relationship that is prone to conflict. What is the *appropriate* division of labour between the state and private capital in society's attempts at economic reproduction? The masterful answers by Smith and Marx to this classic question in political economy did not foreclose further debates on the problem; they merely opened the floodgates. The exigencies of contemporary state-building amidst the military-ideological rivalry of the Cold War era, added new complexities to the age-old problem of the state-business relationship in the 'emerging societies'. In my view, Colin Leys best captured this complexity in his now famous 'Kenyan Debate' (1978), which asked, 'whether or not there are theoretical reasons for thinking that the ex-colonies cannot 'adopt the bourgeois mode of production and develop their productive forces within it'.

The Kenyan debate did so much to nuance the theories of development as they had evolved in the years immediately following the end of World War II. The determinism of the dominant theories of the time, the modernization and dependency theories, was matched by their assumed universal binaries (e.g. tradition versus modern; developed versus underdeveloped), as well as their entrenched teleology. Not surprisingly, the introduction of such mediating variables as the 'nationality' of the bourgeoisie by some development theorists, such as Giovanni Arrighi in the late 1960s, highlighted the need for increased empirical research. While insightful and ground-breaking, Arrighi's (1970, 241) focus on the 'national bourgeoisie' in the developmental equation was limited to 'the implication of the emerging pattern of investment for the national bourgeoisie in nonagricultural sectors'. This was how Arrighi saw the problem:

> The emerging pattern of investment in Tropical Africa creates additional and more powerful obstacles. The rise of an African elite, sub-elite and proletariat proper, enjoying a relatively high standard of living both imposes consumption patterns which discourage accumulation and makes business unattractive relative to salary employment or even wage employment in the capital-intensive expatriate or mixed enterprises.

Leys took the issue several steps further in the Kenyan debate by suggesting that there are reasons other than the profit motive that call for a systematic investigation and eventual empowerment of an indigenous capitalist class in Africa. Unlike Frank (1967), Amin (1973) and their disciples in the Dependency school, who saw capitalist development as simply impossible for the African periphery as long as they remained tied to the rapacious capitalist world system, Leys and his fellow 'rebels' in the self-styled 'classical' Marxist school argued that capitalist development was *mutatis mutandis,* possible and indeed desirable in the African periphery (e.g., Kay 1975; Warren 1980). The intervening variable, according to Leys, was the presence and capacity of indigenous (i.e. African) bourgeoisie. But, why is this so, especially given the general propensity of capital to gravitate to wherever profit potentials exist (i.e. capital logic)? In other words, why should it matter to development whether or not capital was foreign or indigenous? Here, Leys' two-pronged response is profound and audacious, for it dares to open the analytical doors to such explanatory variables as race and patriotism, which are essentially non-measurable and hence useless in economic analysis. First, on the composition of capital, Leys (1994, 229–230) states outright that 'foreign manufacturing capital, organized in MNCs [multinational corporations], is not interested in undertaking or organizing the production of most of its needed inputs [in the periphery], let alone local production in every country where it is established'. Therefore, '[t]o establish the linkages that are necessary to the deepening and extension of capitalist production, *an internal capitalist class is usually necessary*' [author's emphasis]. Second, according to Leys (1994, 230):

> A politically powerful domestic class of capital with an orientation to production is likely to be necessary to secure the political (as opposed to the economic) conditions for the expansion of capitalist production. Otherwise the state is unlikely to sustain the policies needed to resolve the multiple contradictions involved in the process of expanding capitalist relations of production and sustaining capital accumulation in [the] face of opposition from other classes and interests.

Clearly, Leys foresees noneconomic obstacles to capitalist development in the periphery and the possibility that these obstacles could best be mitigated by a coalition of state and indigenous capital. Therein lies the source of Okigbo's *dirigisme.* As he himself had observed with guarded cynicism, between 1972 and 1979, the indigenization programs of the Gowon and Murtala-Obasanjo administrations juridically stripped foreign capital of between 40 to 60 percent of their Nigerian assets, without necessarily increasing local content in the manufactured products. Worse still, the expected transfer of technical and management skills from expatriates to Nigerians workers did not quite materialize. As Tom Forrest (1993, 156), easily one of the most sympathetic students of Nigeria's economic development, has observed:

> There is no reason to suppose, at least in the short-run, that the [indigenization] exercise materially affected the control that foreign capital was able to exercise over corporate enterprise in Nigeria. The relatively wide spread of Nigerian shareholdings usually left the control exercised by blocks of foreign shareholding unaffected. Even though the number of senior Nigerian executives and directors increased, key positions were often left in the hands of expatriates.

Consistent with the central argument of this essay, the primary reason for this observable dysfunction lies squarely in politics. Indigenization was not so much an economic initiative designed to strengthen and further Nigeria's march towards economic development as it was a deliberate political scheme designed to reward the victorious ruling military-civilian elite in the aftermath of Nigeria's civil war. On this, Forrest (1993, 153) is correct in arguing that:

> Commercial pressures to indigenise trade emerged strongly at the end of the civil war with a stronger, more coherent group of traders who had prospered from the civil war. The Indigenous Businessmen's Group in the Lagos Chamber of Commerce attacked the credit policies of commercial banks and the record of the NIDB [Nigerian Industrial Development Bank] for favouring foreign enterprise and argued for more Nigerian equity participation. In 1971, commercial banks were instructed to give 35% of loans and advances to indigenous businesspeople, who also received more favourable foreign exchange treatment from the Central Bank. Such business lobbies found allies among federal civil servants and military officers, who were pressing for increased national control and Nigerian participation in the economy.

Between 1972 and 1980, the various permutations of the indigenization program reflected the struggles and changes that occurred within the odd coalition of the civil bureaucratic elite and their military bosses during the postwar era. In many ways, the crisis of modern Nigeria may be represented as the worst manifestations of the large-scale fraud, which the indigenization program eventually became. The widespread incompetence of the state and private sectors of the Nigerian economy and the attendant corruption and capital flight to western bank accounts are some of the lingering offspring of the indigenization program, the highest level of theoretical attempts in support of the development of an indigenous bourgeoisie that Okigbo had so effectively championed. As fate would have it, he would be called upon in 1994 to expose the massive fraud that his *dirigisme* had produced in Nigeria.

CONCLUSIONS

It is truly remarkable that Okigbo did not succumb to the political harlotry and sycophancy that have been the fate of Nigeria's intellectual elite and political power brokers. If anything, his association with successive Nigerian regimes, both civilian and military, appears to have strengthened his autonomy and sense of obligation to upholding the highest possible standards of public life. He was, after all, a freelance intellectual, who was unencumbered by the institutional constraints of public service. This particular quality may explain his relative autonomy from the crass materialism that has characterized much of the Nigerian ruling class. Okigbo's private consultancy outfit, SKOUP and Company, afforded him an independent means of economic reproduction, thereby freeing him to exercise his mind and express his ideas as he deemed fit. Perhaps, this materialist explanation ignores, like all structuralist arguments do, the role of values he acquired through his training at mission schools, the presence of role models and of legitimate authority structures that enforced norms and rules. As we reflect on the condition of Nigeria's polity today, it is difficult not to wonder why we have allowed a grossly inefficient state to hold society hostage. As I see it, there is no more urgent task today than curbing the pervasiveness of the state in the social, religious, political and economic lives of Nigerians. Today there is little justification for continued state ownership of the media, hotels, banks, factories, airlines and other sundry activities, which are well within the ability of Nigeria's buoyant private sector. In my view, Okigbo's greatest bequest to future generations of policy makers, scholars and public intellectuals may well be a paradigm of empowerment, which is amenable to criticism and refinements for the benefit of *all* Nigerians.

REFERENCES

Amin, Samir. 1973. *Neo-Colonialism in West Africa*. New York: Monthly Review Press.

Arrighi, Giovanni. 1970. 'International Corporations, Labor Aristocracies and Economic Development in Tropical Africa'. In Robert Rhodes, ed., *Imperialism and Underdevelopment: A Reader*, 220–267. New York: Monthly Review Press.

Forrest, Tom. 1993. *Politics and Economic Development in Nigeria*. Boulder, CO: Westview Press.

Frank, Andre Gunder. 1967. *Capitalism and Underdevelopment in Latin America*. New York: Monthly Review Press.

Ihonvbere, Julius. 1994. *Nigeria: The Politics of Adjustment and Democracy*. New Brunswick: Transaction Publishers.

Kay, Geoffrey. 1975. *Development and Underdevelopment: A Marxist Analysis*. London: Macmillan Press.

Leys, Colin. 1994. 'Learning From the Kenyan Debate'. In David Apter and Carl Rosberg, eds., *Political Development and the New Realism in Sub-Saharan Africa*, 220–243. Charlottesville, VA: University of Press of Virginia.

_____. 1978. 'Capital Accumulation, Class Formation and Dependency: The Significance of the Kenyan Case'. *Socialist Register* (London: Merlin Press), 241–266.

Okigbo, Pius N. C. 1962. *Nigerian National Accounts, 1950–57*. Lagos: Federal Ministry of Economic Development.

_____. 1966. 'Criteria for Public Expenditures on Education'. In E. A. G. Robinson and J. E. Vaizey, eds., *The Economics of Education: Proceedings of a Conference Held by the International Economic Association*, 479–494. London: Macmillan Press.

_____. 1965. *Nigerian Public Finance*. Evanston: Northwestern University Press.

_____. 1967. *Africa and the Common Market*. Evanston: Northwestern University Press.

_____. 1981. *Nigeria's Financial System*. London: Longman Publishers.

_____. 1989. *National Development Planning in Nigeria, 1900–92*. London: James Currey.

Sen, Amartya. 2000. *Development as Freedom*. New York: Anchor Books.

Stolper, Wolfgang F. 1966. *Planning without Facts: Lessons in Resource Allocation from Nigeria's Development*. Cambridge, Mass.: Harvard University Press.

Udoji, Jerome. 1974. *Report of the Public Service Review Commission*. Lagos: Government Printer.

Warren, Bill. 1980. *Imperialism: Pioneer of Capitalism*. London: New Left Books.

9

REFLECTIONS ON OKIGBO'S
AFRICA AND THE COMMON MARKET

Una Okonkwo Osili

INTRODUCTION

More than four decades after independence, the future of economic integration in Africa continues to receive attention. Two questions have been revisited: First, can greater integration improve prospects for economic growth and development on the continent? Second, what form should economic cooperation take? These questions appear particularly relevant given the development challenges currently facing the continent.

Until recently, policy makers considered greater regional integration in sub-Saharan Africa as favourable to growth prospects in the region. Several international agencies, including United Nations organizations, such as the United Nations Conference for Trade and Development (UNCTD) and the World Bank endorsed integration initiatives on the continent. New research in this area, however, suggests that the welfare gains associated with regional integration efforts in sub-Saharan Africa may be negligible for medium to long-term time spans (Foroutan 1993). Fine and Yeo (1994) call for a shift in the regional integration paradigm in sub-Saharan towards greater openness to global markets, with less emphasis on the establishment of a common market on the continent. In their view, integration efforts may prove beneficial to growth only if they lead to improved domestic policies and foster investments in physical and human capital.

Pius Okigbo emerges as an important contributor to this debate. As Nigeria's economic advisor to the European Economic Community (EEC) in the 1960s, he faced challenges associated with developing a trade agreement that would secure Nigeria's interests with respect to the EEC, the

Commonwealth and African countries not associated with either of these blocs. His book, *Africa and the Common Market* (1967), summarizes his ideas and is still relevant to understanding the problems and prospects of regional integration in Africa. In the late 1960s, Okigbo drew insights from the trend towards greater integration in Europe and elsewhere in the developing world. Two decades later, his work for the South-South commission represented a recapitulation of his early assessment of common problems facing developing countries. While delivering a lecture on the future of regional integration in Africa in 1990, he concluded that an African Common Market remained a feasible policy goal, and recommended subregional integration as an important first step towards achieving this end (Okigbo 1993).

The objective of this chapter is to assess Okigbo's views on regional integration in Africa and his contribution to the understanding of economic development on the continent. He consistently advocated greater regional integration in Africa, but he also recognized the limitations of such initiatives. He warned that regional integration did not represent a panacea to the economic problems on the continent. Instead, he believed that regional trade arrangements must be pursued alongside efforts to increase Africa's participation in the global economy.

PAN AFRICAN IDEALS VERSUS ECONOMIC REALITIES

In 1963, the Organization of African Unity (OAU) was founded to promote unity and economic cooperation among African states. Eighteen years later, it proposed the *Lagos Plan of Action*, a blueprint for an African common market, a first step towards the eventual formation of an African Economic Community (AEC). The Lagos plan emphasized the subregional integration as an essential foundation for eventual continent-wide economic integration. More recently, OAU has endorsed the idea for the establishment of the AEC by 2005.

The key to understanding the long-standing interest in regional integration in Africa has its roots in Pan-Africanism. Kwame Nkrumah's now famous slogan, 'Africa must unite', captures the optimism of the newly independent states in the 1960s. It was widely believed that regional integration of African economies was critical to achieving greater economic independence and sustainable growth. Furthermore, the drive towards increased inter-African cooperation gained momentum at the height of 'inward-looking' development policies of the 1950s and 1960s. Regional integration was viewed as a means of reducing the reliance of newly independent countries on the industrialized nations of the West, with import-substituting industrialization policies promoted as a major vehicle for economic growth.

Okigbo was educated within the Pan-African tradition. He completed his secondary school education at Achimota College in Ghana, following World War II-related disruptions at Yaba College in Lagos. During this period, he formed close friendships with other West Africans that he maintained throughout his life. A compilation of letters and reminiscences from friends and family published for Okigbo's memorial service further reveals the breadth of his Pan-African interests (The Okigbo Family 2000). Clearly, Okigbo was not only a Nigerian economist, but also a scholar whose experience spanned the entire African continent. A close reading of his writings confirms this view.

Okigbo recognized that efforts towards regional integration were not a novel concept on the continent. Before the twentieth century, long-distance trading networks stretched across the Sahara, connecting West and North Africa to East Africa, Middle East and South Asia. Under alien colonial rule, further attempts were made towards regional integration in Africa, particularly in key sectors such as transport, communication, agriculture, monetary systems, higher education and research. In West Africa, the former British colonies (Ghana, Nigeria, Sierra Leone and The Gambia) shared regional institutions including West African Airways, the West African Examination Board and several agricultural research institutes. Similar efforts were maintained in Southern Africa. In 1917, the East African Common market came into existence with Kenya, Tanganyika and Uganda sharing a common currency, tax administration and systems of transport and communication. Even more important, former French colonies of West and Central Africa were governed as two large federations.

Okigbo understood that new efforts towards achieving greater cooperation and integration among the newly independent African countries would face challenges associated with reconciling different colonial legacies. Furthermore, important distributional consequences would follow regional integration, as some countries would enjoy welfare gains relative to others. According to his view, unless distributional issues could be resolved, benefits from integration, 'would be lost largely because of internal squabbles over the question of unequal gains' among partners (Okigbo 1987, 7).

Okigbo's writings also revealed a deep understanding of Africa's relationships with its trading partners. While some African writers viewed European integration as a threat to African development, he argued that greater economic cooperation in Europe presented 'a challenge, as well as an opportunity' (1987, 104). The opportunities involved maintaining access to

European markets and developing new trading links with economies outside Europe.

ECONOMIC THEORY

Economic theory provides a framework for examining the impact of regional integration on economic welfare. A customs union is defined as an arrangement in which member countries remove trade barriers within the union and maintain a common tariff against non-union countries. Jacob Viner in *The Customs Union Issue* (1950) analyzed the effects of a customs system using the terms 'trade creation' and 'trade diversion'. Trade creation is defined as a shift from high-cost to low-cost sources of supply within the customs union whereas trade diversion refers to a shift from low-cost to high-cost sources of supply within the customs union. When trade diversion exceeds trade creation, then the net welfare gains due to integration will be negative. Under what conditions are welfare gains likely to follow from regional integration? It appears that customs union arrangements are more likely to raise welfare when a high proportion of trade takes place with union countries that maintain a lower proportion of trade with the outside world. For trade creation to dominate, the economies of member countries should be potentially complementary (after the customs union comes into effect).

A close look at current trade patterns among African countries reveals that conditions favourable to trade creation are largely absent. African economies exhibit large noncomplementarities. Most countries are exporters of primary products (crude oil, coffee, tea, cocoa and sugar), goods that are mainly exported to developed countries outside the region. In addition, a large share of manufactured imports like machinery and transport equipment comes from developed countries. Okigbo (1987, 69) recognized that there were limitations to the regional integration schemes so long as the bulk of Africa's trading partners remained outside the region:

> There are many who have asked whether it is really necessary for African countries to forge a special link with the European Economic Community, and whether the answer does not lie in an African Market or perhaps in the type of regional subgroupings that ECOWAS represents.

He maintained that regional integration schemes in Africa could not substitute for trade with the EEC and the rest of the world. New theories of economic growth emphasize the role of scale economies, competition, knowledge and spillover effects (see Baldwin 1997). These ideas have been incorporated into the understanding of the effects of regional integration.

however, it likely that access to markets outside Africa offers the best prospects for reaping the benefits of knowledge, effects of competition and technology transfers.

EMPIRICAL EVIDENCE

Is there still a case for regional integration in Africa? There are serious data problems with assessing the magnitude of intra-African trade, and hence evaluating the impact of greater economic cooperation. Few countries maintain accurate data on trade flows. Furthermore, it is widely recognized that formal statistics, where available, may vastly underestimate cross-border flows of goods and services. This may be of particular relevance to countries where a large share of intra-African trade takes place through informal channels and unpoliced borders. Trade patterns are slow to change. From available data, intra-African trade amounts to a small share of the region's external trade profile. Okigbo's analysis of the trade patterns on the African continent accurately describes present-day conditions. In 1957, the share of intra-African exports in total trade was 16.8 percent, while intra-African imports amounted to 8.5 percent of total trade flows (Okigbo 1967). Between 1989 and 1995, the average share of intra-African exports in total trade fell slightly to 10.3 percent, and intra-African imports rose to about 12.12 percent of total trade.

Consider the example of the Economic Community of West African States (ECOWAS). The economies of the member countries tend to be highly competitive. Many of these countries are located in the same geographic belt and tend to produce similar agricultural commodities. Moreover, manufactured goods produced within the ECOWAS region are produced more efficiently outside the region. In 1980, 2.72 percent of total ECOWAS exports and 3.78 percent of imports originated from other ECOWAS countries, compared to 89.17 percent of exports, and 83.18 percent of imports from the industrialized economies of the West. Thus, patterns of production and demand tend to be oriented towards economies outside the ECOWAS region. The European Union (EU) is the most important trading partner of ECOWAS, accounting for over 50 percent of imports to West Africa, and from which it receives 50 percent of the region's exports. When intra-African trade is examined, we find that trade is concentrated in a handful of commodities and countries. In the 1990s, five countries – Côte d'Ivoire, Nigeria, Kenya, Zimbabwe and Ghana – accounted for about 70 percent of all intra-African exports. In the 1980s, fuels and petroleum products made up about 50 percent of intra-African trade. This share fell to about 30 percent in the 1990s.

The sectors in which significant change in intra-African trade has taken place have the greatest potential for intraregional trade expansion. In the late 1960s, Okigbo (1967, 143) predicted that food and textiles were likely to represent important categories in the future of this trade. His expectation has been borne out by the work of Yeats (1998), who provides a list of 30 categories of goods that have experienced high growth rates in intra-African trade since the 1980s. By examining these new exports, it is possible to determine the directions in which intraregional trade is likely to expand. Specific sectors such as food processing, chemicals, wood, manufacturing and textiles represent significant sources of growth in intra-African trade. In particular, foods and feeds have emerged as important categories in intra-African trade, making up 25 percent of regional exports. Among the fast-growth exports, four countries (Zimbabwe, Kenya, Ghana and Cameroon) account for 22 of these new export goods. Machinery and transport equipment, Africa's main imports are not yet represented as a potential growth area in intraregional trade.

OKIGBO'S CONTRIBUTIONS

Why was Okigbo committed to the eventual realization of an African common market? Certainly, the record of subregional integration in Africa has been far from promising. Over 200 organizations are dedicated to promoting cooperation in the region; however, the agenda of regional organizations have remained largely unfulfilled. Although numerous treaties have been signed, member states have implemented very few agreements. With few exceptions, intra-African trade continues to account for only a small share of official overall trade on the continent. Many African countries display undiversified export profiles, with a high degree of dependence on a small number of primary products. An additional problem in evaluating the likely impact of greater regional integration is that current schemes have been poorly implemented. In many African countries, customs duties are an important source of government revenue. In 1987, for example, they represented over 60 percent of government income for The Gambia, Lesotho and Uganda (World Bank 1989) and over 30 percent of incoming revenue for Burkina Faso, Liberia, Senegal, Sierra Leone and Togo. Thus, the fiscal implications of trade liberalization reduce the willingness of governments to embark on the implementation of regional agreements. In addition, infrastructures for transportation and communication within subregions remain underdeveloped.

Through an analysis of Okigbo's writings, it is possible to understand why he supported regional integration initiatives, despite the dismal record of progress in this direction in the years after independence. His endorsement of regional integration within Africa relied on three main arguments: economies of scale, the constraints of geography and the importance of human and physical capital for economic growth. He argued that country size represented a major obstacle to growth. At independence, many African countries were small, economically undeveloped states with limited infrastructures. Fifteen countries in sub-Saharan Africa (among them Guinea-Bissau, The Gambia, Lesotho and Gabon) had populations of less than 2 million. Trade restrictions and political boundaries influence the extent of the market. He maintained that country size conferred economic ad vantages, allowing large countries to exploit scale economies in production.

Does country size actually confer economic benefits? Okigbo (1987, 388) contended that for 'nations of small size or awkward location', economic integration might improve prospects for economic growth. Africa has a large number of land-locked countries. Thus, regional cooperation in transport and communication may prove important in reducing transport costs for greater participation in global markets. Recent work in macroeconomics draws attention to country size and its role in economic growth. Alberto Alesina, Enrico Spolaore and Romain Wacziarg (2000) present evidence that demonstrates how country size positively affects economic growth, with the extent of the market measured by the total income or population.

A related question is whether regional integration can help African countries over-come the limitations of market size. Here, the evidence is mixed. The emerging consensus is that openness to trade, rather than regional integration efforts will improve economic growth outcomes. Jeffrey A. Frankel and David Romer (1999) also find that openness to trade improves growth performance. The experience of some East Asian countries, commonly referred to as the Asian Tigers, provides valuable lessons. Although many of these countries have small internal markets, outward orientation through the promotion of exports to global markets has enabled them to expand beyond their domestic markets. Regional integration through the Association of South East Asian Nations (ASEAN) may not have played an important role in the rapid economic growth of these economies (World Bank 1993), but it does highlight the problem of geography.

Moreover, Okigbo understood that long-term economic growth prospects in Africa depended on investments in health and education. The development of a skilled work force required mobilization of resources at both the subregional and regional levels. He recognized that regional cooperation in research, particularly in agriculture and high-technology areas, might be necessary because capital resources and skills are scarce on the continent.

BEYOND GAINS FROM TRADE

To date, the gains from cooperation in Africa have been discussed in the relatively narrow confines of benefits from customs unions and other types of trade agreements. Given the poor record of regional integration efforts, it may be critical to explore other sectors that may benefit from greater cooperation at the continent-wide level. Two recent developments deserve attention. In April 2001, African leaders convened in Abuja, Nigeria for the Africa Summit on HIV/AIDS, Tuberculosis and other Related Infectious Diseases. It may be too early to assess the impact of greater cooperation among African leaders on the prevention and treatment of HIV/AIDS; however, the control of river blindness in West Africa relied on regional cooperation, and demonstrates that such cooperation in health care can yield considerable benefits (World Bank 1989). In their recent work, Kremer and Miguel (2001) identify important externalities associated with health interventions in Africa. Thus, greater policy coordination in the areas of education, research and treatment may reduce the negative welfare effects of HIV/AIDS on Africa's population.

The second area in which regional initiatives have met with partial success has been in peacekeeping efforts on the continent. In 1993, ECOWAS added regional peacekeeping objectives to its mandate. Through its military observer group, ECOMOG, ECOWAS has played a prominent role in seeking resolution to conflicts in Liberia and Sierra Leone. Several countries on the continent are presently embroiled in internal political conflicts, and there may be a role for regional organizations and continent-wide bodies in resolving these conflicts.

CONCLUSION

I now return to questions posed at the beginning of this chapter. Given current trade patterns, it is unlikely that greater regional trade integration will lead to large improvements in welfare in sub-Saharan Africa. Access to global markets may be more beneficial to economic growth. Although global markets have increased in their openness, Africa's share of the world trade has fallen. In the mid-1950s, sub-Saharan Africa accounted for 3.1 percent of global exports, but the continent's share fell to 1.2 percent in the 1990s. Thus, trade policies on the continent may have a role to play in increasing Africa's participation in the global economy.

Pius Okigbo's research and views on trade policy contribute to an ongoing debate on the link between regional integration and African development. An important argument developed in his writings held that the benefits of cooperation at the regional or continent-wide level might not be limited to trade agreements. Regional agreements and policy coordination in investments in transport and communication, technology, education, health and securing political stability on the continent may prove beneficial in improving growth prospects in Africa.

REFERENCES

Alesina, Alberto, Enrico Spolaore and Romain Wacziarg. 2000. 'Economic Integration and Political Disintegration'. *American Economic Review* 90(5):1276–1296.

Baldwin, Richard E. 1997. 'Review of Theoretical Developments in Regional Integration'. In Ademola Oyejide, Ibrahim Elbadawi and Paul Collier, eds., *Regional Integration and Trade Liberalization in SubSaharan Africa*, Vol.1, 24–88. New York: St. Martin's Press.

Fine, Jeffrey and Stephen Yeo. 1997. 'Regional Integration in SubSaharan Africa: Dead End or Fresh Start'. In Ademola Oyejide, Ibrahim Elbadawi and Paul Collier, eds., *Regional Integration and Trade Liberalization in SubSaharan Africa*, Vol. 1, 428–474. New York: St. Martin's Press.

Foroutan, Faezeh. 1993. *Trade Reform in Ten Sub-Saharan African Countries: Achievements and Failures*. Washington, D.C.: World Bank.

Frankel, Jeffrey A. and David Romer. 1999. 'Does Trade Cause Growth?' *American Economic Review* 89(3):379–399.

Okigbo, Pius. 1967. *Africa and the Common Market*. Evanston, IL: Northwestern University Press.

———. 1987. 'Africa and a Changing Europe: Hopes and Fears'. Lecture at the Royal Institute of International Affairs. In Pius Okigbo, ed., *Essays in the Public Philosophy of Development*, Vol. 5: *Studies in the Political Economy of Africa*. Enugu: Fourth Dimension Publishers.

Okigbo Family. 2000. *An Extraordinary Life: Tributes to Dr Pius Okigbo (1924–2000 A.D.)*. Onitsha: privately printed.

Viner, Jacob. 1950. *The Customs Union Issue*. New York, Carnegie Endowment for International Peace.

World Bank. 1989. *Sub-Saharan Africa: From Crisis to Sustainable Growth*. Washington DC: World Bank)

———. 1993. *The East Asian Miracle: Economic Growth and Public Policy*. New York: Oxford University Press.

Yeats, Alexander J. 1998. 'What Can Be Expected of African Regional Trade Agreements? Some Empirical Evidence'. Washington, DC: World Bank, Development Research Group (Trade).

10

WEST AFRICAN INTEGRATION AND THE EUROPEAN UNION: THE FUTURE OF THE CFA FRANC.

Souleymane Bachir Diagne

Pius Okigbo wrote *Africa and the Common Market* in 1967. Now, over thirty years later, we need to draw from the rich legacy left by Okigbo by questioning the future of that relationship through looking at his study, *Africa and the Common Market* (1967). In this work, he shows very well how the association of African countries to the Common Market started as an 'accident', a pure continuation of the colonial ties between some European countries and their former African territories. As a matter of fact, towards the end of the negotiations for the Treaty of Rome that set up the framework for the Common Market, France decided at the last minute that the affiliation of six of her former African colonies to this new European institution must be a condition for her participation. With reluctance, the other five countries (among which three—the Netherlands, Belgium and Italy—were also former colonial powers) accepted. Then, after what Okigbo calls 'The crisis of Independence and the problem of Renewal', a larger association was designed to bring in the countries from 'the other Africa', the English speaking ones. Some of the latter countries entered into negotiations so half-heartedly, that it was not surprising that the talks fell through. Nigeria did negotiate an agreement in 1966, but it was not ratified. Kenya, Tanzania and Uganda followed suit with the Arusha agreement of 1969. Radical African leaders, led by Kwame Nkrumah of Ghana, however, viewed such alliances as ultimately working against the unity of the continent by fostering vertical ties of the African countries with Europe that were detrimental to the horizontal ties they desired to develop among themselves.

At this point, one can raise the question of the monetary union as a foundation for African unity. This is what I wish to do in this paper, focusing on the *Communauté Financiaire Africain* (CFA) franc zone.

Many sub-Saharan African politicians and financial experts are keenly interested in the launching of the euro, the new currency of the European Union (EU), in the beginning of 2002. The future of what is known as the CFA franc zone, a grouping of West and Central African countries, is at stake. These countries share, as part of their French colonial heritage, a common currency, called the CFA franc, which is guaranteed by France. In West Africa, eight countries make up the *Union Monétaire Ouest-Africaine* (UMOA): Benin, Burkina Faso, Côte d'Ivoire, Mali, Niger, Senegal, Togo and since April 1997, Guinea Bissau, the only country with no historical ties to French colonial rule. In Central Africa six countries constitute the *Communauté Economique et Monétaire d'Afrique Centrale* (CEMAC)): Cameroon, Central African Republic, Congo-Brazzaville, Gabon, Equatorial Guinea and Chad as well as The Comoros. Outside these two zones, other countries are involved in the process of regional integration all over Africa, a process that may involve the adoption of a common currency. How this might come about is unclear and the focus of heated debates. Perhaps the CFA zone might be expanded or new Pan-African currencies might be instituted.

France has assured its former colonies that the launch of the euro in 2002 will not mark the end of the special relationship between the French treasury and the CFA franc monetary zone. Of course, the other Common Market countries have agreed to this stipulation, but until when? This is a crucial question, given the largely unpredictable dynamics towards unification that are going to develop in Europe as well as in Africa. In April 2001, during the eleventh meeting of the ministers of finance of the franc zone, the assurance concerning the permanent linking of CFA to the new European currency was reiterated. On the one hand, Charles Konan Banny, current governor of the *Banque Centrale des États de l'Afrique de l'Ouest* (BCEAO) (Federal Bank of West African States) has expressed the bank's intention to keep the situation going while at the same time, he has insisted that the African countries concerned must foster efficient methods of economic management. On the other hand, French minister Laurent Fabius has repeated that the parity between the euro and the CFA will remain fixed and has called for the reinforcement of legal measures against money laundering (see *Le Soleil* 2001b).

Beyond the purely technical mechanisms through which this zone could maintain for a while its special ties with the EU via France, and beyond the purely economic and commercial consequences of this agreement, there are other fundamental questions to consider. Questions about identity and sovereignty or community and autonomy must be raised by Africans, who need to reflect upon their own situation and future not only vis-à-vis Europe, but also in a world characterized by global movements, especially those that are creating new and larger transnational and transcontinental unions in the intermediate spaces between the nation-state and the open world.

For example, what is the meaning of the CFA franc in terms of identity for the CFA franc zone countries? Certainly, this is an important question. From 1945 to 1994, that is to say for two generations, the CFA currency has maintained the same value vis-à-vis the French franc (FF), namely 1FF for 50 CFA. This could be seen as the long lasting result of the colonial heritage. Some countries determined to break this colonial tie with France. For example, after independence, Mali and Mauritania were eager to create their own currencies, a manifestation of sovereignty and an affirmation of one's economic and cultural identity. Does that mean that the CFA zone could not invest, so to say, the identity of its people in the currency (bearing all the images and symbols expressing African cultures)? The answer is not simple. It must be said that, given the long length of time during which the CFA was accepted as a stable international currency, African populations nevertheless found ways to appropriate the currency within their cultural purview. Various populations gave their own names to the currency in their own languages. They twisted the counting of it and changed the basic units, thus mobilizing the resources of the logic embodied in their native-tongues. Such assertions bear witness to *cultural identification*.

Let me illustrate this point by referring to the way in which this appropriation occurred in my native tongue: Wolof. Wolof is quite unique among West Atlantic African languages in that it has evolved a decimal system of counting. That is to say, there was *a priori* no problem at all for immediate translation of monetary operations in the language, using one franc as the unit. But it turned out that the basic unit used is five francs instead of one. Now when one looks at the name for five francs, '*dërëm*', it is clear that this is a *Wolofization* of the Arabic word *dirham*. This probably occurred as the result of Islamization and the establishment of Islamic law, for in Islam certain amounts of money have a precise legal import (dowry, for example) calculated in *dirham*. The equivalence between the franc and the *dirham* became accepted, with the result that five francs for a *dirham* was adopted as a monetary unit. The final result was, and this is the point I want to make, that under the decimal logic of the franc currency, *the Wolof have designed a system of their own*, in which their own computation of the *dërëm* has taken precedence. Thus, they both culturally and symbolically created their own currency within or under the CFA currency, a process of genuine *appropriation*.

The devaluation of the CFA franc in 1994 marks a major break, not only financially and economically, but also psychologically and culturally. Beyond the economic consequences of the devaluation, a major outcome was the destruction of the identification produced by the use of the currency for decades. Even the way in which the decision was taken, mainly by international financial institutions and by France's ministry of cooperation, came as a shock, for the African presidents of the states concerned had all clearly expressed their opposition. It brought to clear light the fact that ultimately the CFA currency is an instrument controlled by foreign hands. Also – and this is important – it became evident that sharing a common currency did not mean true economic solidarity for the African countries in the zone. They were not integrated *horizontally*. Each was integrated *vertically* towards the world market, and thus separately, just as Nkrumah had warned so many years before.

On the symbolic level, after the devaluation, there was a shift in power and social meaning from the CFA to the French currency itself. With regard to the issues of identification and appropriation, we must examine the symbolic meaning and social role a currency has in a community. Recently, a very interesting article in the Senegalese daily, *Le Soleil*, published an excellent report on the expectations, hopes, anticipations and fears of populations living in southeastern Senegal as they contemplated the economic and social consequences of the replacement of the French franc by the new euro (*Le Soleil* 2001a). This is the part of the country most concerned with emigration, mainly to Europe. Because of the money sent by emigrants in France, the French currency now circulates more widely than the local CFA franc. Wealthy returned immigrants are building houses, stores and other structures and paying for them directly in French francs, the currency that represents and expresses in no uncertain terms their achievement, wealth, and, ultimately, power. The currency has been incorporated as a particularly powerful symbol in the traditional ways of displaying social status, especially on social occasions like marriages, baptisms and funerals. This symbolic and social meaning explains why the populations have developed quite a unique relationship to the French currency and are looking forward to what is going to happen now to that relationship with the new European currency. Often reports show genuine nostalgia for what appears to some persons as the loss of what had been 'the symbol of France's grandeur since General De Gaulle'. The most widespread attitude, however, is the belief that the euro will simply fulfil the same type of symbolic function as the present French franc.

Meanwhile, another possible regional currency seems to be in the process of creation, and this might initiate a new process of true identification with a common West African currency. With increasing globalization, Nigeria, Ghana, Sierra Leone, Liberia and Guinea are deliberating the formulation of a regional currency, one of the early objectives of the Economic Community of West African States (ECOWAS), founded by fifteen countries in 1975. Currently, mainly the Anglophone members are attempting to create a common currency as part of the West African Monetary Zone (WAMZ) (see *This Day*, March 15, 2002). The obvious next step should be for ECOWAS countries to amalgamate the two currencies of the region (see *The Herald*, March 13, 2002). In any case the role of a democratic Nigeria, ready to assume its natural leadership in the region, will be crucial. I believe that Pius Okigbo pioneered such a role for Nigeria within a truly united West Africa.

REFERENCES

Herald (Harare). 2002. 'Region makes New Push for Monetary Union'. March 13.

Okigbo, Pius N. C. 1967. *Africa and the Common Market*. Evanston, Northwestern University Press.

Le Soleil (Dakar). 2001a. 'Passage à l'Euro dans l'Est du Sénégal: peu d'angoisse, un brin d'émotion'. April 28.

———. 2001b. 'La Zone franc préoccupée par l'avènement de l'Euro fiduciaire. 11ème réunion des ministres des Finances de la Zone franc à Abidjan'. April 28.

ThisDay (Lagos). 2002. 'Obasanjo Launches Sensitisation Programme on Monetary Zone'. March 15.

PART IV: INTELLECTUALS, PUBLIC LEADERSHIP AND CIVIL SOCIETY

11

THE POLITICS OF PUBLIC INTELLECTUALS UNDER ABACHA AND AFTER

William Reno

The sociologist Max Weber wrote that responsible statecraft requires 'relentlessness in viewing the realities of life, and the ability to face such realities and to measure up to them' (Weber 1958, 120). The proposition that rulers are answerable for their policies and that citizens judge them according to their conduct is captured in the popular terminology that rulers hold 'positions of responsibility'. The expert, or public intellectual, is central to this exercise of power and responsibility. Pius Okigbo (1986, 1) provided us with his own definition of that mission that captures this connection between expertise and the public interest. 'The expert should be able to formulate the options open to Government', he reminds us. 'They should make their knowledge available to the Government in fullest detail, and to the public in as much detail as it can digest' whether they are part of a government or occupy a purely independent position.

'The "experts" and "specialists" to whom society would naturally look to furnish answers have lost the sense of who and what they are as integral tissues of mankind in history', complained Arthur Nwankwo (1990, v). Critics observe that Nigeria's political system exercises a magnetic attraction to public intellectuals. This tendency became especially pronounced during the notorious Sani Abacha regime (1993–1998). Some experts presented their views to please politicians rather than provide critical evaluation of policy. Such tendencies caused the economic historian Walter Ofonagoro (1996, 2008–2010), who served as Abacha's Information Minister, to declare: 'There is no opposition; every Nigerian is with us. This is the achievement of Abacha's administration.' It is to be expected that a government's ministers will support that government, but declarations of society-wide solidarity in the face of massive repression implicates one in destructive policies. The sociologist Peter Ekeh identified this tendency as part of a 'dual morality' that splits Nigeria's public and private spheres of life so that the scramble for wealth and power overshadows the pursuit of moral life and community norms in the public sphere, even while public sycophants and corrupters continue to behave in a morally upright manner in the context of family and friends.

Are Nigeria's public intellectuals implicated in misrule to an unusual degree when compared to public intellectuals in other countries and if so, is this development unique to Nigeria? Ekeh (1990, 660) has argued that the spread and reinforcement of kinship ties and other forms of clientelism dating back to Nigeria's precolonial history hinder the development of independent critiques of those in power. Moreover, collaboration represents a form of self-defence against a violent state that is unable to protect or advance the interests of its citizens. But such a broad conception, while containing important truths, does not explain the simultaneous and continual appearance of independent criticism and analysis from public intellectuals, even in difficult times. Outspoken intellectuals such as Chike Obi, the world-renowned mathematician who proved Fermat's Last Theorem, have remained life-long political activists (Obi 1986). Aliu Babs Fafunwa (1990, 1998), once a minister of education, continues to advocate the importance of vernacular language education. The geographer Akin Mabogunje (1976), erstwhile head of the Development Policy Centre, addresses weaknesses in national policy formulation and generates proposals for reform (Mabogunje and Obasanjo, 1992). Numerous other Nigerian intellectuals have provided perceptive critiques of officials in power and their policies – often at great personal risk – whether from direct government repression in the past or running afoul of treacherous political cross-currents now.

What are the features of Nigeria's political system that attract some public intellectuals and repel others? I describe and explain this process in terms of a particular style of rule that coopts critics and experts. This style of rule intentionally promotes violence and coopts experts to disorganize and demoralize the population. The country's top rulers have accomplished this through employing formal bureaucratic institutions and policies for purposes other than what these institutions were originally designed. Lacking any coherent program of social transformation or economic growth, past regimes have intentionally cultivated the behaviour and policies that experts have identified as key causes of political and economic crisis. In political terms, this type of politics is a kind of nihilism, since it does not articulate a realistic ideological or programmatic framework. Rather, it ignores the interests of those it rules and does not seek broad approval or cultivate legitimacy from among the wider population.

Nonetheless, disorder is effective as a political instrument because it divides opponents and discredits potential challengers who become compromised through their complicity with oppressive regimes. This is designed to taint political debate and reduce the capacity of political ideas, political parties, or even individual politicians (or would-be politicians) to address basic social and political issues or build broad-based followings. The obvious association of some public intellectuals with corrupt regimes cheapens their pronouncements and proposals, which contributes to popular cynicism. Ideals then become politicized as propaganda and do not carry as much weight as they would otherwise. Consequently, enterprising people who aspire to easy fame and power become eager to subscribe, even if they have no intention of doing something worthwhile. As the enterprising businessman and politician Arthur Nzeribe advised the ambitious, 'If everybody in Nigeria was corrupt, he would be a fool to be an exception to the prevailing rot and malaise' (cited in Osifo-Whiskey 2000, 3). This is a system of rule that does not seek approval from citizens. Nonetheless, it is a rational strategy for holding onto power in the sense that it does cater to the private interests of members of regimes and suppresses challenges.

For prominent individuals attempting to escape this corruption, emphasis on primary identities, especially ethnic and religious communities, is one of the few ways of erasing complicity with past regimes. Yet this strategy poses the long-term risk of destroying Nigeria as a single polity. In spite of this pessimistic view, the brief examples above show that some public intellectuals continue to voice opinions critical of officials as well as address what most people recognize as basic social and political issues. Their behaviour demonstrates that short-term rational choices and personal aggrandizement upon which officials have depended do not guide all political action. Given the legacy of several decades of corruption and misrule, their presence has be-come especially important as a bulwark against the disintegration of Nigeria. Their example offers different choices in politics and social reconstruction.

PRUDENCE AND THE PUBLIC INTELLECTUAL

Recently, fashionable notions such as 'civil society', though enamoured with electoral exercises and multiparty competition, really speak to the universal belief that political communities are also moral communities. The idea that rulers should be responsible to this morality is embodied in the popular term 'public servant' as used to refer to politicians and policy-makers, and 'public interest' to refer to the core interests of the communities that live within the state. Rulers may be tempted to ignore public interest in favour of a preoccupation with his or her political fortunes. This is a common short-coming of rulers everywhere, including democratic ones. Nonetheless, it is the moral quandary of all politicians who wish to be accepted as legitimate by those whom they rule that they must balance their personal desires with a capacity to identify and respond to a public interest. Public interests may defy public opinion and entail higher taxes, for example, or perhaps require compulsory military service for the sake of long-term security or stability. Public intellectuals, as Okigbo describes them in his words above, are central to the education of public opinion and the definition of public interests and ultimately the legitimacy of rulers. It was the wilful absence of these interests during the Abacha administration and in other Nigerian regimes that has shaped how it coopted intellectuals and manipulated violence as strategies of power. This absence of reciprocity in relations between ruler and ruled also gives public intellectuals a very different, and I will argue below, more important role than that which they occupy in most other countries.

Central to this notion of public interest and the role of public intellectuals is prudence, which Edmond Burke called 'the first of virtues in politics' (quoted in Bredveld and Ross 1967, 38). Prudence is the human injunction that arises whenever substantial power and thus significant hazards are involved, or where values important to communities are at stake. 'The leadership of the country is what the driver is to the car', explains General David M. Jemibewon (retired) (1998, 348). The prudent driver checks on the condition of the car, learns what is necessary to keep it running, and obeys at least some rules of the road (out of personal interest, not just concern for pedestrians and other drivers). Likewise, people in positions of political power and high office also have to be alert to hazards and surprises. Politics and administration calls for attention caution and care. Contrasting his description of Igbo society with the interests of Nigeria's rulers at the time, Okigbo (1986, 18) notes that it is this sort of prudence that holds together societies throughout history. The essence of statecraft in Eastern Nigeria, as in most societies, lies in its support for the qualities that people admire such as the fruits of hard work, achievement, integrity and fidelity. He detects, however, a lack of interest in wider Nigerian political circles for support of these values, a rejection that extends to a similar lack of interest in the advice of experts. This produces an 'aristocracy of wealth' that overshadows what was once an 'aristocracy of knowledge', resulting in the subordination of expertise in the civil service to the dictates of short-term political calculation (Okigbo 1986).

THE ABSENCE OF PUBLIC INTEREST IN THE GOVERNMENT
Wole Soyinka (1986, 14–15) captured the gulf between notions of public interest and personalist rule in Abacha's time with his statement that:

Abacha has no *idea* of Nigeria – Abacha has no *notion* of Nigeria. He is thus incapable of grasping what is being said to him by some entity that speaks with the resolute voice of the Civil Liberties Organization, the Campaign for Democracy, the National Democratic Coalition, the market women, civil servants, student unions, labor unions, the press and so forth.

But the fact that Abacha had no notion of Nigeria in the sense of conceiving of it as a public realm and in separating his private interests from statecraft did not mean that Abacha was incapable of ruling the country, at least in terms of controlling it and suppressing what he viewed as threats to his personal hold on power. This manner of (mis)rule is central to understanding the fate of public intellectuals in his regime and the special role they play in post-Abacha Nigerian politics.

Abacha's style of rule, while more extreme in example, followed a pattern developed during Babangida's presidency from 1985 to 1993. It was not the case that Abacha and his predecessor were unintelligent or irrational, even if not terribly articulate. Babangida ruled in the context of the failed Vatsa (1985) and Orkar (1990) coup attempts, events that may have played a key role in shaping the character of his own rule. Likewise, Abacha, as a participant in several coups, then head of his own seizure of power in November 1993, understood the insecurities facing regimes in Nigeria. Not all rulers who use violence to come to power become obsessed with their personal security. Figures such as Burkina Faso's Thomas Sankara (1983–1987) and Nigeria's own Murtala Muhammed (1976) relied upon populist appeals to mobilize supporters, though the lesson to others is that both of these men were killed by close associates.

Babangida and Abacha were not alone in Africa in facing threats to their regimes. By 2000, over half of Africa's states had experienced violent regime transitions. Through the 1970s and 1980s rulers could anticipate a 72 percent chance that they would be violently removed from office. Based on data in *Keesings Record of World Events*, this percentage fell to 41 percent in the 1990s as more countries held multiparty elections. Nonetheless, rulers in many states still face serious challenges to their hold on power. In 2000, for example, Algeria, Angola, Burundi, Democratic Republic of Congo (formerly Zaïre), Republic of the Congo (Brazzaville), Guinea-Bissau, Sierra Leone, Somalia and Sudan – nine of Africa's 52 states – hosted major armed struggles against incumbent regimes. Six of these conflicts included elements of national armies that had revolted against ruling presidents (Sollenberg and Seybolt 2001, 53–55). Even among the six countries holding multiparty elections in 2000, opposition parties boycotted in two (Sudan and Côte d'Ivoire), an opposition leader died under mysterious circumstances (Guinea-Bissau) and another campaign aggravated separatist violence (Tanzania).

The immediate response of many politicians, who do not enjoy acclaim from their own citizens, including military rulers in Nigeria, who themselves came to power through violent means, has been to undermine institutions and organizations that either are, or could become, arenas for criticism and opposition. This response targets public intellectuals, whether they respond to government policies or not, since rulers often regard the independent organizations that house them as actual or incipient threats to the security of their hold on power. At the very least, independent criticism of policies highlights the possibility that alternatives may exist, and popular critics of government could emerge as viable challengers. A primary official reaction has been to undermine and close down these institutions, either through cuts in funding to official institutions, or direct repression. A more effective, and in the long-term more damaging strategy, has been to coopt and taint intellectuals and advisors so that their pronouncements and criticisms will be greeted with cynicism and disrespect by the population.

Abacha's administration did not hesitate to employ direct coercion to silence especially vocal critics. Broad-based trade unions and national profess-sional organizations that were capable of articulating and publicizing alternative economic and political strategies received the brunt of official repress-sion. Individuals such as Claude Ake, who resigned from the official Niger Delta Environmental Survey project, also posed special challenges to government when they raised central political issues. Ake, for example, left the official survey to pursue his own analysis of the politics and social impact of the oil economy, which had provided the Nigerian government with revenues of $183.1 billion between 1970 and 1988. Before his untimely death in an airplane crash, Ake called for a national debate about oil, one of the most basic and widely recognized elements of Nigeria's national life, explaining 'What is at issue is nothing less than the viability of Nigeria, as oil is the real power and the stuff of politics in Nigeria' (Ake 1997, 6). Implicit in this analysis (and explicit in Ake's writings) was a call to renegotiate the overall relationship between the federal government, the states and ethnic communities. The hanging of Ken Saro-Wiwa and his associates in 1995 also reflected the urgency of Abacha's administration to suppress challenges to the foundation of its power, and by extension, any real legitimate debate about oil.

While the brutal elements of official repression attracted international attention, more subtle strategies of cooptation and redirection of the energies of public intellectuals proved effective at limiting challenges to Abacha's power. While the suppression of national organizations such as the Academic Staff Union of Universities (ASUU) removed a major organizational framework for articulating criticism, the proliferation of single-issue nongovernmental organizations (NGOs) helped to occupy experts with tasks of mitigating the social consequences of misrule. Commendable though the actions of organizations such as human rights groups and community development initiatives may be, 'the question of what to do invariably has a lot to do with how adequately these groups are to set a framework for action' (Jega 1999). These organizations keep people busy with important tasks and searching for funding, but they may also reduce attention to connections between local problems and the wider political analyses of experts like Ake. Consequently, they fail to become the broad-based political vehicles that trade unions and professional organizations once were.

Even while Abacha's administration created plenty of economic and social problems that NGOs sprang up to address, Abacha and his associates used the mask of reform policies to root out other potential sources of challenge to his rule. All of these 'initiatives' entailed recruiting technocrats and expert advice, though with no intention of actually acting on the advice. The image this was meant to impart was not one of competence or progress. Instead, its aim was to show the remoteness of real reform in a country where experts, preferably known critics, were seen as squandering their standing in exchange for privilege.

The Failed Banking (Recovery of Debts) Decree No. 18 of 1994 should be considered in this context. Its application represents a clever manipulation of expert advice from within Nigeria and abroad over concern about the solvency of Nigeria's banking system. Earlier, Babangida's administration presided over the expansion of major financial institutions from 41 in 1985 to over 120 in 1993. This expansion reflected their own manipulation of reform policies to generate patronage opportunities and wealth for Babangida's clique and their political allies (Akanbi 1996). Babangida's and then Abacha's behaviour clearly subordinated the role of expert advice in administration. As one bank inspector complained (after the murder of several colleagues critical of new banking practices): 'This job has a lot of professional risks! It is hazardous. We just pray that God protect us!' (Ode 1996, 25). This approach to financial sector 'reform' on the part of lower level civil servants shows that the problem of mismanagement and corruption in Nigeria is not one of cultural attitudes, or that Nigeria's bureaucracies are inherently corrupt, but instead that the impediments to real reform are political problems. In fact, what is remarkable here is that at least some civil servants brave substantial hazards to do their jobs, despite pressures from their superiors to do otherwise.

Predictably, organizing banks and granting banking licenses according to political criteria undermined Nigeria's banking system. Yet probes of bankers after 1994 continued to subordinate expert advice to political criteria. Targets for probes and prosecution included Hakeem Bello-Osagie, head of United Bank of Africa (UBA), one of Nigeria's more solid financial institutions. Others facing probes such as investment banker Oladotun Duro-Emmanuel of Group Merchant Bank explained that he and other bankers were targeted because they supported Chief Moshood Kasimawo Olawale Abiola, who was elected on June 12, 1993 but was never to take office. He explained further 'We were too independent and did not need to come to Abuja to seek contracts, patronage, approvals and whatever from the Presidency. He [Abacha] must control everything to stay in power and there was a need to destroy private wealth', an attitude towards societal autonomy that was consistent with the Abacha administration's hostile approach towards such public intellectuals (Matthew 2000, 4). Abacha's actions constituted misrule in technocratic and moral terms of providing for the public interest. Nonetheless, they were part of a rational overall strategy of consolidating Abacha's hold on power, which was aimed mainly at eliminating all sources of challenge, including all provocative ideas, not just threatening individuals.

The second component of the strategy involved cooptation of public experts. Anthony Ani, Abacha's finance minister, explained that the failed banks decree was part of a strategy to 'increase government capacity to introduce transparency' (*Africa Confidential*, June 23, 1995, 2). The fact that Ani's statement received some positive consideration among Nigeria's foreign creditors and helped legitimate Abacha's actions – at least in foreign eyes – underlines the extent to which the seduction of experts was not limited to Nigeria's shores (*Africa Confidential*, November 3, 1995, 2–3). The expert in charge of the Nigeria Deposit Insurance Corporation, however, was Ibrahim Sani Abacha, the son of the president. Neither a banker nor a trained accountant, Ibrahim Abacha played a major role in selecting bankers for prosecution, implicating Ani in this process. Targets of these probes also alleged that the junior Abacha had personal motives, primarily targeting those who refused pressure to sell shares of businesses to the Abacha family.

Cooptation of experts and the absorption of the whole notion of reform into Abacha's political strategy provided him with a valuable political resource. Some bankers who were targeted indeed were corrupt, and it was generally recognized that the damage that Babangida's earlier 'reform' inflicted on Nigeria's economy called for remedial measures. Therefore Abacha could pose as a fighter against corruption. As one journalist wrote, 'the masses are happy with the failed banks tribunal and the idea that there is no sacred cow in society' (Olaniyonu 1996, 8). For those taking more critical views there was the spectre of members of Nigeria's administrative and academic elite joining Abacha in this process. For example, Abacha's early cabinets included personalities such as Olu Onagoruwa, former leader of the

Movement for National Reform as attorney general. As an expert in press law, Onagoruwa (1986) was especially knowledgeable about what constituted violations of press freedom, even as he served as Abacha's chief prosecutor.[1] Despite his expertise, Onagoruwa presided over suppression of press freedom as is well documented in Nigeria in *Constitutional Rights Journal* and *Media Rights Bulletin* and by agencies outside of Nigeria. Abacha's appointment of fake 'experts' such as Umaru Dikko, a man whose name became synonymous with corruption during the Second Republic, to a constitutional conference had the additional effect of debasing this basic political exercise and reinforcing connections in the popular imagination between civilian government and extreme corruption (K. Soyinka 1994).

Other appointments were aimed at discrediting the unseated civilian president Abiola's associates. The appointment of Abiola's vice-presidential running mate, Babangana Kingibe, as secretary for international affairs aimed to demoralize and weaken the unity of opponents. The appointment of the lawyer-turned-journalist Ebenezer Babatope as transport secretary underscored the weakness of ideological opponents, as Babatope (1981, 1986) was a critical expert on the anatomy of coups and advocate of ideological alternatives to military rule.[2] The plethora of special commissions, presidential initiatives and government supported 'NGOs' provided channels for coopting other less luminary or more shy experts and critics. Exercises such as Vision 2010 and Africa 2020 provided a veneer of interest in technocratic management and were staffed with various experts. Abacha announced that Vision 2010 (the chairman of which was Chief Ernest Shonekan, whom Abacha forced from power in November 1993) would 'look at everything, the education system, crime, agriculture... Vision 2010 will continue far-reaching measures to sanitize the system and instil some discipline in the operation of the economy and public management' (Report of the Vision 2010 Committee 1997, 55).

The contradiction in such proposals becomes apparent when one considers the fate of Nigeria's commercial bankers who failed to privilege political demands made upon them rather than the demands of business competitiveness and profit. Vision 2010 could never promote economic growth for political reasons; to do otherwise would be to increase independent wealth that could be used as a base from which to criticize Abacha and

---

[1] Onagoruwa authored *The Nigerian Civil War, Fundamental Human Rights, and International Law* (1970) and *Press Freedom in Crisis: A Study of the Amakiri Case* (1986).

[2] Babatope's radical views are delineated in his books, *Coups: Africa and the Barrack Revolts* (1981) and *Nigeria — The Socialist Alternative* (1986).

organize opposition. It was thus worse than Soyinka's assertion that Abacha lacked a sense of public service. Not only did Abacha have *no idea*, *no notion* of Nigeria in terms of serving a public interest, Abacha simply had no interest in serving a public interest even if he understood what public interest meant in an abstract or administrative sense. This basic political distinction put Abacha in the same category of rulers such as Zaire's Mobutu Sese Seko, Liberia's Charles Taylor, Zimbabwe's Robert Mugabe and Sierra Leone's Siaka Stevens, each of whom eventually subordinated statecraft to the maintenance of personal power and wealth. Ignoring the advice of independent experts, they systematically destroyed institutions and informal political channels for articulating alternative policies and in doing so, subjected their countries to economic decline and political violence.

Abacha's subordination of public interest to his private project of holding power and getting rich was a powerful taint on those who collaborated with this project, and a source of great public cynicism about these 'experts'. Abacha's style of rule also highlights the extent to which Nigeria under his control was not a 'weak state' in an overall social sense of being able to control the opposition of citizens. Instead, the informal social control of cooptation and subsequent discrediting of experts and public intellectuals went far towards disorganizing opposition. Nigeria did become a weaker state in a formal institutional sense. But as noted above, this had political benefits too, since misrule in a technocratic policy sense left the country with few bureaucracies in which efficient managers could develop their own perspectives, critiques and followings, or the opportunity for beneficiaries of successful economic programs to use their private wealth to finance critical expertise. Impoverished intellectuals and trained professionals had few other options but to serve in officially supported institutes or to found NGOs that could take government contracts to feed their families and maintain some financial comfort amidst economic crisis. Thus, government could employ experts in fake exercises to apply 'expertise' to these problems. This presents an image of consultation and accountability, but in fact implicates participants in the policy failures that they ostensibly are charged with remedying.

SOCIAL CONTROL AND THE SHAPE OF OPPOSITION

The systematic delegitimation of experts and critics impoverishes Nigeria's political opposition. Citizens have no incentive to take even sincere critics of government seriously when they have seen so many critics in the past switch positions for the sake of some material benefit. The legislative head of a major opposition party in the post-Abacha period lamented: 'The majority of us cannot go home. You drive your NASS (National Assembly) car on the streets and people shout "thief, thief"' (Onyeacholem 2000, 18). Politicians and those associated with government continue to have to contend with active efforts of recycled and long-lived politicians and sycophants attached to Nigeria's previous regimes to link anyone with new ideas with corrupt and immoral behaviour of the past. This is not, however, a straightforward process. For example, Arthur Nzeribe's formation of a committee to urge major parties to acclaim Obasanjo as their standard bearer for the 2003 presidential election easily recalls Nzeribe's campaign of his Association for a Better Nigeria (ABN) on behalf of Babangida as the sole candidate for election in 1993 (Benson and Akinola 2001, 11–13). Barely a year earlier, Nzeribe had headed a move to impeach President Obasanjo! That Nzeribe is also a senator in the federal legislature implicates this body in his machinations. Obasanjo might get off with being perceived as a victim of Nzeribe's tactics, but the damage is done. Citizens might easily, and for the most part, accurately conclude that all politicians are similarly without principle. The political benefit for Nzeribe and those who back him lie in opportunities that they may find in political turmoil as they bring the institution of the senate into disrepute (as the behaviour of this and other assemblies provide critics with ample ammunition), further choking off legitimate channels for the articulation of political alternatives.

Meanwhile, non-official, informal political channels that remain free of these negative associations gain greater respect. In the midst of the impoverishment of public discussion of ideas, however, organizing around broad ideological and policy alignments becomes very difficult to sustain in a setting where so many public figures appear to choose positions on the basis of short-term personal calculations. Even well meaning policy makers and their critics will be suspected of harbouring ulterior motives. Consequently, anything government does will not attract widespread legitimacy among the public, at least not initially, even if people derive real benefits. As the Nzeribe case shows, Nigeria's political parties will not soon become vehicles for mobilizing citizens around a reformist agenda. Instead, music events, football clubs and other informal venues become more important as vehicles for political criticism and organization. Youths may respect the political wisdom of Bob Marley or Fela more than that of an expert or critical politician. They may see more consistency and honesty in the latter's *International Thief Thief* and his Kalakuta Republic, where he lived in relative modesty, despite his wealth. People who are very angry about Nigeria's sorry state take him seriously when they hear him sing 'suffer, suffer for 60 sitting, 90 standing', even though he was rich enough to buy fleets of cars and did not need to travel on overcrowded buses. More to the point, he refused invitations to write praise-songs for politicians or to sing at private parties where he might be 'sprayed' with money. This real autonomy allowed him to achieve the status of public intellectual and expert, because he could convincingly point out and explain the reasons for the failures of government on basic issues in a manner digestible to the public.

Other informal channels for mobilizing opposition are less benign, yet more prevalent because of the political environment that the impoverishment of public discourse creates. They include violent gangs, campus cults and radical religious, ethnic and nationalist groups. Poor people, especially unemployed youths, could not get coopted because they are of such low status that they would have little to offer to political patrons, except to work as armed muscle for politicians. For those of higher status, radical nationalism serves as a means of either erasing, or ensuring that other people do not suspect complicity with past regimes. The militant communal politician can put distance between himself and the incumbent administration, since most regimes associated most explicit exclusionary ethnic appeals with the dissolution of Nigeria and suppressed them. In a situation in which most well-known people were either associated with discredited regimes or faced repression, and in which political philosophies and ideologies were never taken seriously, violent gangs and radical nationalists really do offer new ideas and strategies that can be used to oppose corrupt rulers. These ideas and strategies also are the easiest ways for enterprising young people new to politics to mark out power positions.

This new nationalism and youth protest usually has very little ideological content since those who normally articulate broad political aims in most opposition groups in most societies are either complicit or suspected of being complicit (or harbouring hopes of lucrative cooptation) with the country's political elite.[3] For enterprising individuals, whether new to the political scene or attempting to cleanse themselves of the taint of previous associations, these tactics become the quickest means to distinction. But to do so, they must shed the old suspect language of the public intellectual or policy critic. This variety of opposition does not need the public intellectual. The experience of the past teaches them that reflection is equated with weakness and emasculation. Instead, their organizations prize action for action's sake. They exhibit a poverty of speech and elementary syntax, all the more useful for limiting complex and critical reasoning.

Recent developments show that politicians use violent gangs to cleanse themselves of previous associations and stake out positions in opposition to the current regime. Anambra State Governor Mbadinuju's support for the Bakassi Boys, a heavily armed group of youths, enabled him to pose as a foe

---

[3] An exception to this is found in political Islam. Critics like Ibrahim el-Zakzaky maintained consistent records of opposition to Government and resistance to efforts to coopt them. They also possess the benefits of a widely known and comprehensive framework for critique in the Holy Quran, a source relatively impervious to cooptation by Abuja.

of corruption and anticrime activist, regardless of his real record. Like many young Nigerians, these youths are inspired by the armed military interventions of leaders like Yoweri Museveni in Uganda, Paul Kagame in Rwanda and the multinational African force that kicked Mobutu out of power in Zaire (now Congo). In a popular move, Mbadinuju invited Bakassi Boys to rid the state of armed robbers, and in 2000 bestowed upon them the official title of Anambra State Vigilante Services, a paramilitary directly under the control of the governor's office (Agekameh 2000, 23–27). Mbadinuju also claimed that Bakassi Boys operated as an anticorruption unit, and sought to associate himself with this crusade.

In fact, the Bakassi Boys threatened to kill an Anambra State legislator whom they and Mbadinuju claimed was corrupt. The governor justified the Bakassi Boys' actions, saying:

> They came to me and said they have been looking for this man [the legislator], and that they had gone to his house to catch him because he [the legislator] committed criminal offences and I said no matter how highly placed a person is, anyone who is suspected of being an armed robber, we will bring him out and test him, so they [the Bakassi Boys] tested him [the legislator] as they normally test everybody and he didn't meet up with the test (Onwubiko 2000, 11).

It also underscored the political tension between Mbadinuju, with his own political ties to the past, and Obasanjo's People's Democratic Party. The episode above also enabled the governor to remove (and almost kill) a political opponent in the state legislature under the guise of fighting corruption. Later, the murder of the Anambra State head of the opposition All People's Party (APP) at the hands of the Bakassi Boys removed another political opponent of the governor's. This move resulted in a more sustained federal crackdown on Bakassi Boys. Meanwhile, the governor could position himself as an advocate of citizens' rights to defend themselves against crime. Through appropriating the language of anticorruption, he could justify Bakassi attacks against opponents whom he said 'showed undue loyalty to some 'money bags' who had sworn to destabilize state government', rather than inviting people to examine his own record (Eke 2000, 8).

It also shows that individual politicians now have proven able to adapt the violent methods and cooptation strategies that the Abacha regime reserved for itself to defend their own position. The long-term danger is that politicians will use what start out as popular vigilante groups to address a real crime problem as private armies to fight political battles and gain access to economic opportunities. This private use of violence may come to dominate a broader federal-state power struggle. If it does, it will mirror the fragmentation of patronage politics in places like Liberia, Somalia and Congo, where state elites took advantage of popular cynicism and anger towards rulers and the growing availability of private violence to carve out their own political fortunes and wealth. Doing so, however, required that these recycled politicians hitch their fortunes to a new appeal, usually one with a healthy dose of communal chauvinism.

Campus violence has emerged as a microcosm of official efforts to redirect protest in society at large. Previously not known for violence, 'campus cults' appeared in the 1980s at the same time that university unions and associations critical of Babangida's administration faced official repression, culminating in the outlawing of the National Association of Nigerian Students (NANS) in 1986 and the removal from classrooms of professors (public intellectuals such as Julius Ihonvbere at the University of Port Harcourt, Bala Usman at Ahmadu Bello University (ABU) and Patrick Wilmot (also at ABU), who were critical of the government. Officials gave support for 'peace movements' at the University of Ibadan and Obafemi Awolowo University to undermine student activism. In the northern part of the country security agents infiltrated fundamentalist religious groups to set them at odds with secular radicals (Falola 1998).

Security agencies used these armed gangs to demobilize university-wide and national student political movements. At the University of Nigeria (Nsukka), for example, a police-sponsored vigilante group launched 'Operation Zero Option' in 1988 when students planned to protest petrol price rises. More recently, students at the University of Ibadan alleged that violent campus cults there received support from the university's administration to attack students who gathered to discuss political issues (Adeleke 1999, 24). Campus cults enlist not only those who battle fellow students for control over student unions and other institutions; they also recruit individuals who may simply wish to settle scores with rivals or take advantage of disorder to get loot.

Meanwhile, radical nationalist groups such as the O'dua People's Congress (OPC) have become important alternative vehicles for mass protest, in part feeding off of this militarization of youth. In contrast to the Bakassi Boys' anticorruption and anticrime appeals, the exclusionary ethnic appeals of the OPC's radical wing has offered followers a more independent critique of Nigeria's politics since it articulates a position that many politicians consider harmful to Nigeria's continued existence. 'Our primary objective', stated Kayode Ogundamisi, the OPC national secretary, 'was to canvass a sovereign national conference that will lead to an autonomous Yoruba nation' (Tunji 2000, 15). While a moderate wing of the OPC has been more willing to work with the Obasanjo government, even this group favours the wholesale renegotiation of southwestern Nigeria's relationship with the rest of the Nigerian federation. Like the Bakassi Boys, however, OPC leaders can tap grassroots support through fighting corruption. They express widespread public opinion in Lagos, more often reflected in popular videos and songs than in the official media, that 'behind armed robbers are influential people in the society, including police officers who themselves are beneficiaries of robbers' exploits' (Agekameh 2000, 25). This gives OPC members a degree of legitimacy among youth who admire the stand taken against great risk to oppose Abacha's rule. This also gives OPC leaders more autonomy to articulate their own political program since they do not rely upon the patronage of politicians to gain visibility before the public eye, leaving them better able to act as an ethnic militia, attacking other groups that they believe have taken undue advantage of their stranger status to enter trades or settle in particular areas.

V.P. Gagnon (1994–1995, 125–52) makes the important observation in the context of former Yugoslavia that violent opportunism results in what he calls 'political homogenization' that crowds out less violent, less self-interested political discussion. This process complicates the efforts of would-be public intellectuals to articulate a political agenda, since increasing violence tends to force otherwise passive individuals to seek protection from armed groups. In Nigeria, as in former Yugoslavia, political violence in the absence of strong organized political alternatives offers enterprising local strongmen opportunities to carve out their own fiefdoms and settle local scores under the cover of mass violent protest against an old order (Nwankwo 1997). It is a small step for them to organize this culture of violence into its more brutal practice.

THE ROLE OF PUBLIC INTELLECTUALS IN POST-ABACHA NIGERIA

The relationship between rulers and societal groups in Nigeria, with its abundant expertise with markets, bears some resemblance to former communist regimes. While Nigeria never made cement or steel so well as socialist countries (as the failed Ajaokuta aluminium smelter shows), its rulers have proven quite effective at destroying broad-based social movements and atomizing and isolating public intellectuals. Indeed, Nigeria's recent rulers have been effective in achieving this goal, when compared to Poland's solidarity movement and the Soviet Union's tenacious national environmental and anticonscription movements, especially in the Ukraine and Russia, in the late socialist era. These organizations played important roles in constructing successor regimes in postsocialist states, and where they were absent (or where enterprising nationalist politicians intentionally targeted them, as in former Yugoslavia), the cohesion and viability of the state itself has been uncertain with people expressing their frustrations through violence.

Thus Nigeria's public intellectuals have a crucial role to play not only in building a democratic political system in Nigeria, but also in preserving Nigeria from the fate of Sierra Leone, Liberia and other places where old regimes systematically destroyed broad-based autonomous social organizations and discredited experts and reformers. Out of these violent situations rose armed groups with divisive ideological or political programs to take revenge on those whom they hold responsible for injustice. In the long run, public intellectuals and others, who are able to critique government from positions of independent authority often become role models from whom both officials and ordinary people take their cues. This relationship with the rest of society goes beyond simply trying to prevent abuses of power in the hope that if one can do this, everything else will be all right. The people must insist that government officials and others perform creatively to ensure the well-being of the whole society.

Shortly after the newly elected General Olusegun Obasanjo (retired) assumed his position as president of Nigeria, he appointed the Human Rights Violations Investigation Commission, chaired by retired Supreme Court Justice Chukwudifu Akume Oputa, to look into past human rights violations in Nigeria. This still remains one of the dividends in democracy designed to publicize crimes of past regimes and address abuses of past administrations. It has done little, however, to promote the affirmative possibilities for public intellectuals. Roughly modelled along the lines of South Africa's Truth and Reconciliation Commission (TRC), the Oputa Commission is charged with investigating disappearances, extrajudicial executions, torture and assassinations and other abuses from January 1966 to June 1998. But this commission operates with few funds and is overwhelmed with applications – over 10,000 from Ogoniland alone. It has no authority to compel witnesses or defendants to testify and cannot offer immunity or amnesty in return for truthful testimony. For example, on the basis of new information the commission ordered the head of Abuja's police to reopen the investigation into the death of Obi Wali, a former Senate minority leader, a request that the police ignored.

More damaging has been the Oputa Commission's tendency to steer clear of the most important figures from the past, most notably Babangida himself. It will be very difficult for political activists and public intellectuals to work within the framework of Nigerian democracy if day-to-day politics becomes consumed by speculation concerning the 2003 presidential aspirations of this or that recycled politician, or the machinations of people like Arthur Nzeribe, noted above. Meanwhile, the persistence of campus cults and private armies of local strongmen, such as the Bakassi Boys, pose the risk of further delegitimating the current regime as people become cynical about its capacity to provide order, much less hold a meaningful and non-violent 2003 election.

In this context it is understandable that many Nigerians would find a more basic and wide-ranging political negotiation to be desirable, since it would address central political questions such as the nature of federal-state relations, the uses of oil revenues and the role of religion in Nigeria's political life. Such an exercise also would be more likely to provide a more neutral venue in which public intellectuals can articulate alternatives and voice criticisms. Probably it is only through such a radical break with past practice that people can be convinced that their rulers will pursue public interest, and that there will be room for the prudence in the running of the affairs of the country that Pius Okigbo championed in his work and life.

REFERENCES

Adeleke, Lanre. 1999. 'The Attack Was Sponsored'. *Tell*, July 26:24.
Africa Confidential. 1995a. 'Battle for the Banks'. June 23:2.
———. 1995b. 'Investing for Tomorrow'. November 3:2–3.
Agekameh, D. 2000a. 'War of the Killer Gangs'. *Tell*, June 12:25.
———. 2000b. 'Blood Law of the Bakassi Boys'. *Tell*, August 28:23–27.
Akanbi, Raimi, ed. 1996. *Redasel's Companies of Nigeria*. Lagos: Research and Data Services.
Ake, Claude. 1997. *Why Humanitarian Emergencies Occur: Insights from the Interface of State, Democracy and Civil Society*. Helsinki: United Nations University/World Institute for Development Economics Research.
Ani, Anthony. 1978. *Companies Income Tax and Petroleum Profits Tax in Nigeria*. Ibadan: Oxford University Press.
Anonymous. 1986. 'Sorcerers, Astrologers and Nigerian Economic Recovery'. Kuru: National Institute for Policy and Strategic Studies.
Babatope, Ebenezer. 1981. *Coups: Africa and the Barrack Revolts*. Enugu: Fourth Dimension Publishers.
———. 1986. *Nigeria: The Socialist Alternative*. Benin: Jodah Publishers.
Benson, Dayo, and Wale Akinola. 2001. 'My Deal on Obasanjo — Nzeribe'. *Sunday Vanguard*, April 22:11–13.
Bredveld, L. I., and R. G. Ross, eds. 1967. *The Philosophy of Edmund Burke*. Ann Arbor: University of Michigan Press.
Eke, E. 2000. 'Crisis is Part of Anambra State'. *The Guardian on Sunday*, October 29:8.

Ekeh, Peter. 1990. 'Social Anthropology and Two Contrasting Uses of Tribalism in Africa'. *Comparative Studies in Society and History*, 32(4):660–699.

Fafunwa, A. Babs. 1990. *Up and On! A Nigerian Teacher's Odyssey.* Lagos: West African Book Publishers.

———. 1998. *Memoirs of a Nigerian Minister of Education.* Lagos: Macmillan.

Falola, Toyin. 1998. *Violence in Nigeria: The Crisis of Religious Politics and Secular Ideologies.* Rochester: University of Rochester Press.

Frynas, Jedrzej George. 2000. *Oil in Nigeria: Conflict and Litigation between Oil Companies and Village Communities.* Hamburg: Lit Verlag.

Gagnon, V. P. 1994–1995. 'Ethnic Nationalism and Internal Conflict: The Case of Serbia'. *International Security*, 19(3):125–52.

Jega, Attahiru. 1999. *Leadership Factor in Nigerian Trades Union Movement and World Historical Experience.* Lagos: Dr. M. E. Kolagbodi Memorial Foundation.

Jemibewon, J. D. 1998. *The Military, Law and Society.* Ibadan: Spectrum Books Limited.

Keesings Record or World Events, 1995–2002. London: Keesing's Limited.

Mabogunje, Akin. 1976. *Cities and African Development.* Ibadan: Oxford University Press.

———, and Olusegun Obasanjo, eds. 1992. *Elements of Democracy.* Abeokuta: African Leadership Foundation (ALF) Publishers.

Matthew, Kayode. 2000. 'How Abacha's Family Ruined Us'. *Vanguard*, November 30:4.

Nwankwo, Arthur. 1990. *African Dictators: The Logic of Tyranny and Lessons from History.* Enugu: Fourth Dimension Publishing Co.

———. 1997. *On the Brink of Disaster: Nigerian Ethos and the Meaning of the Tragic State.* Enugu: Frontline Publishers.

Obi, Chike. 1986. *Our Struggle: A Political Analysis of the Problems of Peoples Struggling for Their True Freedom.* Enugu: Fourth Dimension Publishers.

Ode, Joseph. 1996. 'Bankers behind Bars'. *Newswatch*, March 11:25.

Ofonagoro, Walter. 1976. *The Currency Revolution in Southern Nigeria.* Los Angeles: University of California.

———. 1979. *Trade and Imperialism in Southern Nigeria 1881–1929.* New York: Nok Publishers.

———. 1996. 'What Abuja Thinks'. *West Africa*, December 23:2008–2010.

Okigbo, Pius N. C. 1986a. *In the Public Service.* Enugu: Government Printer.

————. 1986b. 'Towards a Reconstruction of the Political Economy of Igbo Civilization'. Ahiajoku Lecture. Owerri [Imo State, Nigeria]: Culture Division, Ministry of Information, Culture, Youth and Sports.

Olaniyonu, Yusuph. 1996. 'Does Abacha Plan to Exit in 1998?' *TheWeek*, July 15:8.

Onagoruwa, Olu. 1986. *Press Freedom in Crisis: A Study of the Amakiri Case*. Ibadan: Sketch Publishing Company.

Onwubiko, E. 2000. 'Why Obasanjo Unbanned *Bakassi Boys*, by Mbadinuju'. *The Guardian*, August 30:11.

Onyeacholem, G. 2000. 'This House Stinks'. *Tell*, September 4:18.

Osifo-Whiskey, Onome. 2000. 'Nzeribe's Brinksmanship'. *Tell*, May 1:3.

Sollenberg, M., and Taylor Seybolt. 2001. 'Major Armed Conflicts, 2000'. In *SIPRI Yearbook 2001: Armaments, Disarmament and International Security*, 15–64. New York: Oxford University Press.

Soyinka, Kayode. 1994. *Diplomatic Baggage: MOSSAD and Nigeria, the Dikko Story*. Lagos: Newswatch Books, Ltd.

Soyinka, Wole. 1996. *The Open Sore of a Continent*. New York: Oxford University Press.

Tunji, B. 2000. 'Why We Are Fighting, OPC Secretary'. *The Guardian*, July 22:15.

Vision 2010 Committee. 1997. *Report of the Vision 2010 Committee. Main Report*. Abuja: Federal Republic of Nigeria.

Weber, Max. 1958. 'Politics as a Vocation'. In H. H. Gerth and C. Wright Mills, eds., *From Max Weber: Essays in Sociology*, 77–128. New York: Oxford University Press.

12

DEVELOPMENT AND IDENTITY: FRAMING THE SOUTH-SOUTH DIALOGUE

Kalu N. Kalu

Whichever way we look, we are at a loss, and so we are forced to do what seems also to be the safest thing – that is, to speak our minds at all costs. For, situated as we are, words left unspoken might occur to us afterwards and upbraid us with the thought that, if spoken, they might have saved us.
–Thucydides, *The Peloponnesian War.*

And speak, they did. The general issue of economic and developmental asymmetry between the developed countries of the North and the under-developed countries of the South, or what we generally term as the Third World has occupied much of the discourse on North-South relations. In this context, the framework for South-South cooperation was meant to grant a unified voice, character and identity in its continued dialogue with the North. The primary obligation for the South therefore, was to conduct an internal assessment of its capabilities and weaknesses, and to see how much of that can be leveraged to advance its stakes in a very fluid and dynamic global environment.

In 1955, the Afro-Asian Conference at Bandung was the first indication of the entry of a self-conscious South into the world arena. Later, the founding of the Non-Aligned Movement in 1961 and of the Group of 77 in 1964 marked the start of collective action by the South to advance its corporate interests. Still it took the formation of the South Commission in 1987 to initiate a multinational and multidimensional approach in dealing with the crisis of economic development that has been the bane of the South for many years. The commissioners contemplated that this effort would help to arrest the shortcomings of earlier South-South cooperation, characterized by a lack of institutionalized technical support and a failure to reflect the objectives of mutual cooperation in national plans and policies.

This chapter has three objectives. First, it will explain the South Commission as an ad hoc framework created to engage both the theoretical and practical issues relevant to the development of the South, and its consequent evolution as the South Centre. Second, it will discuss the role of Pius Okigbo as a member of the South Commission, but more pointedly his contribution to the North-South economic discourse as well as to the institutional ideals of the South Centre. Third, it will situate the recommendations of the South Commission within the orthodox liberal paradigm generally advocated for developing countries.

THE SOUTH COMMISSION: CHARTING IDENTITY AND VOICE

In the effort to address the developmental problems of the countries of the South, it became imperative to examine the fundamental issues in a comprehensive manner, despite the unique circumstances that may pertain to some countries. 'In the prevailing environment, South-South cooperation offers developing countries a strategic means for pursuing relatively autonomous paths to development suited to the needs and aspirations of their people' (South Commission 1990, 16). Some opinion leaders also held that by exploiting the opportunities created by cooperation, the South as a group could strengthen its position in negotiations with the North. Following years of informal discussion among intellectual and political leaders from the South on the necessity for a South Commission, Prime Minister Mahathir Mohamad of Malaysia spearheaded the final initiative in 1986 after a meeting organized in Kuala Lumpur by the Third World Foundation and the Malaysian Institute of Strategic and International Studies. At the Non-Aligned Summit Meeting in Harare in September 1986, the prime minister announced the intention to establish the commission as both an intergovernmental organization and as a policy advisory and advocacy agency for the collective interests of the countries of the South, essentially to operate as a 'think tank'. In 1987, the commission was formally inaugurated as an independent international commission, with Julius Nyerere, former president of Tanzania as its first chairman.

Members of the commission were chosen from the various countries of the South. They received no payment. They undertook work in the commission in their individual capacity, not as representatives of their governments or institutions, even when they held official positions. The commission succeeded in raising an initial sum of seven and a half million dollars through donations to begin its three years of work. The donations came mainly from countries in the South, but some northern countries also subscribed. The government of Switzerland authorized the commission to set up its secretariat in Geneva as an international organization and awarded a three-year subsidy to cover rent and office overhead. The commission commenced operations on August 1, 1987; held its first official meeting in Mont Pelerin, Switzerland, on October 2–5, 1987; and its last meeting took place in Arusha, Tanzania, in October 6–8, 1990. In all, the commission held eight plenary meetings before submitting its report, *The Challenge to the South*, in August 1990.

The terms of reference for the commission's work were delineated at its second meeting in Kuala Lumpur on March 1–3, 1988, and included the following points:

1. Analysis of the national development experience in the South;
2. Analysis of the global environment;
3. South-South cooperation for collective self-reliance;
4. North-South relations.

Twenty-eight commissioners were appointed to the commission, including Aboubakar Diaby-Quattara from Ivory Coast, Gamani Corea from Sri Lanka, Enrique Iglesias from Uruguay and Pius Okigbo from Nigeria. The members were drawn largely from Africa, Asia, Latin America and the Pacific Islands, but also included Yugoslavia, which was then an active member of the Non-Aligned Movement. In the effort to get a grasp of the enormity of the task ahead of it, the commission set up 20 expert working groups to consider, among other things, the Uruguay round of negotiations on the general agreement on tariffs and trade (GATT), commodities, North-South issues, science and technology, the United Nations system and development indicators and strategies. During its three years of operation, the commission issued separate statements on two pressing issues: external debt and the GATT trade negotiations.

In its final report, the commission assessed the South's achievements and failings in the development field and suggested directions for action. Although much of this work was undertaken in the final years of a decade in which many economies in the South were devastated, the report strikes a note of hope and makes a cogent case for self-reliant, people-centred development strategies. It also shows how developing countries could increase their strength and bargaining power through mutual cooperation. Describing how global arrangements for trade, finance and technology handicap the South, it urged the countries of the South to act in solidarity in the multitude of North-South negotiations. It also argued that growing global interdependence benefited all peoples, providing developing countries with a better chance to escape poverty and attain sustainable development. Nonetheless, it acknowledged that the ideal of self-reliance should not obscure the reality that development policies in the South also depend on an improvement in its relationship with the North. Hence it stated that 'the issue for the South is not whether to cut its links with the North, but how to transform them. The relationship must be changed from exploitation to shared benefit, from subordination to partnership' (South Commission 1990, 211).

With regard to the final report of the South Commission, Okigbo was not specifically mentioned as a member of any particular working group of the commission. Rather, his role was essentially interlocutory as a conciliator of ideas and programmes among a series of working groups that considered particular development problems. While at first this might seem a general observation, one must look much deeper to see how central his contributions were both for the South Commission and the South Centre.

OF THINKERS, TRAVELLERS AND RAINMAKERS
In order to understand fully the role of Okigbo from the formative stages of the South Commission to the establishment of the South Centre, one has to take an intellectual excursion into some of his literary works. He was a prodigious writer, but it was not until I encountered his five-volume collection, *Essays in the Public Philosophy of Development* (especially Volume 4), that I realized how much his vision, philosophy and macroeconomic insights helped to shape both the ideology and the moral argument for South-South cooperation as well as set the framework for the work of the South Commission. In fact, one can see that much of the argument presented in the South Commission's report was predicated on views delineated in his *Essays* – in some cases cited verbatim. Many of these essays were written before the inauguration of the South Commission. We may also see this development in his correspondence and exchanges with the South Centre secretariat in Geneva. In these essays and exchanges, three main ideas stand out.

Redeeming the Self in Service. Early in 1987 Nyerere and Okigbo met in Lagos after a prominent Nigerian of 'international' renown had recommended the latter to Nyerere. They discussed the purpose of the proposed commission and shared ideas about the problems of and opportunities for development in the South, and in Africa in particular. Before they separated, Okigbo had, in response to a question posed by Nyerere, indicated that if asked, he would be prepared to serve on the commission. Not long afterward, in July 1987, he was invited to be one of the seven African members of the commission. Nyerere was to serve as chairman.

As some of Okigbo's associates in both the South Commission and the South Centre have observed, he did not engage in extensive debates nor did he make lengthy statements. Although he never rushed to speak at any of the plenary meetings, his fellow commissioners soon recognized that he carefully studied the papers and considered the contributions of his colleagues before speaking. His interventions were always judicious, coming at strategically important junctures in the discussions when his precise remarks promoted the evolution of consensus and collective thinking. Of particular long-term significance were his interventions during the two concluding meetings of the commission in Caracas and Havana where his views contributed to the decision to establish a two-year follow-up transition programme rather than end its work abruptly. Eventually, this crucial decision led to the setting up of the South Centre in Geneva as a permanent successor to the ad hoc commission. Nyerere was invited to be its foundation chairman. Obviously, this meant an intense fund-raising campaign, and Nyerere at first hesitated to undertake more years of constant travel and financial worry; however, Okigbo, supported by two other commission members, persuaded him to head the new organization.

During this transition period, Okigbo helped to organize the West African presentation of the South Commission's report, *The Challenge to the South*, as well as its local publication in Nigeria. Converting the South Centre into a permanent institution proved to be a slower and more complicated task than originally expected. Negotiations had to be set up with the Swiss government about the continuation of the centre's small secretariat. Moreover, arranging consultations with leaders of developing countries about the centre's form and constitution was time consuming. Nyerere appointed Okigbo to the advisory committee, which formulated policy during the transition, but never actually met on a formal basis. Throughout this period, Nyerere consulted Okigbo regularly concerning the new organization's structure and objectives.

When, in 1995, the South Centre was legally established as both an intergovernmental organization and a policy advisory and advocacy agency for the collective interest of the countries of the South, Okigbo was selected to serve on its nine-member board. In addition, he served on the three-member subcommittee dealing with the investment of the centre's capital fund. The board met, on average, twice a year but contact between the members and the chairman or the secretariat was much more frequent than that. As his health deteriorated during the last three years of his life, he was not able to attend every board meeting or play as active a role as he had during the planning of the South Commission. Yet he remained in constant communication with Nyerere until the latter's death on October 14, 1999. The two men not only respected each other's ability and commitment to the future of Africa; but they also liked each other and enjoyed working together. Okigbo completed one three-year term on the board of the South Centre, and was re-elected for a second. His death on September 12, 2000, less than a year after Nyerere died, brought to an end a life of committed service to improve the quality of life of Africans and other people enmeshed in poverty throughout the South.

Crafting a Public Philosophy of Development. With respect to the work of the South Commission, Okigbo was an idealist more than a techno-crat. His intellectual insights, as explored in his *Essays in the Public Philosophy of Development*, were instrumental in forging the ideological anchor for South-South cooperation and North-South dialogue. His main thesis was that 'development is about man, the whole man, and not about artefacts of living or material things'. For him, development centred on human beings, integrating beliefs about culture and religion with the acquisition of knowledge, modes of production, distribution, consumption, investment, politics and environment. The more total the integration achieved, the more balanced would be development. He maintained that: 'Development will have meaning only if there is sufficient limitation on the exercise of power, democratic sharing and participation in the scope of that power, and full respect for the rule of law that applies to the high and the low simultaneously' (Okigbo 1993, vol.2, 234). The system must allow the full play of the energies of the people within set rules that apply to all equally and fairly. But to the extent that each society has its own way and its own rate of adaptation to a new environment, Okigbo acknowledges, 'the problem of designing a new development paradigm is how to work these principles into the new theory of development'. He sustained an abiding belief that government must play an active and decisive role in bringing about the development of a scientific and high-tech society as well as in human capital development:

> It cannot be left entirely to the play of market forces. The creation of incentives, the promotion of an intellectual infrastructure, the upgrading of the scientific community, are some of the areas where the government, and it alone, can intervene effectively (Okigbo 1993, vol. 2, 237).

While this may be an attempt to show the link between socioeconomic inequality and the prevailing form of economic organization, this view is also consistent with the argument that in 'purely capitalist systems, the ever-growing gap between rich and poor — 'the haves and the have nots' — invariably promotes increasing inequality in political resources' (Hadenius 1992, 103). To the extent that 'the market offers only private "solutions" to collective problems...this can generate a conflict with such strong outbreaks as to lead to the collapse of political democracy' (Bates 1981, 87, 103). Okigbo clearly distinguishes between the traditional conception of development and its alternative for developing countries. He argues that while there exists a clear case of material growth in the affluent North, it is also possible to have growth without development. What the developing countries desire is the need for planning, a full mobilization of their human and physical resources and the will to attack a number of critical bottlenecks simultaneously. Even as 'new bottlenecks emerge, the resolution of one set of major bottlenecks will throw light on the method for resolving the new ones' (Okigbo 1993, vol. 3 198–199).

The Macroeconomics of Collective Action. As indicated earlier in this chapter, the South Commission's report dealt with many issues germane to South-South cooperation and development. The three issues that have always stood out, both in the report and elsewhere, were external debt, poverty and self-reliance. The commission's stance on these issues clearly incorporated Okigbo's views, especially as articulated in his lecture, 'The Gains and Pains of Structural Adjustment' presented to the Lagos Chamber of Commerce and Industry on September 28, 1988, about two years prior to the conclusion and submission of the commission's report (Okigbo 1993, vol. 4, 198–199). In that lecture, Okigbo laid out his views as well as approaches on how to deal with the ramifications of external debt as nations struggle to implement their structural adjustment programmes. Pointedly, he asked: Is it possible to reduce the stock of debt and the service charges? Regarding this question, he argued that while some countries have taken the neutral course of rescheduling their debt year-by-year, thereby shifting in time the burden of service payment and transfers, eventually, such an approach would raise the total stock of debt.

These ideas greatly influenced the South Commission's strategy for dealing with the issue of external debt, which recommends that the stock of debt must be reduced in the following way. He proposes that first, it can be reduced by cancelling some of it, and in part, by revaluing the commercial debt to bring its nominal value in line with the market value. Second, debtor countries should not be made to bear the brunt of the changes in the financial obligations arising from arbitrary fluctuations in interest rates in the industrial countries, changes for which they cannot be held responsible. Third, the various options for dealing with the service charges should be consolidated to offer the best menu to the debtor countries, coupled with a long moratorium of at least six to ten years. Fourth, debtor countries should convene a forum to pool their ideas and their strengths and demand that the creditors completely reorganize debt portfolios, bringing them in line with a debtor country's earning capacity and possibilities for growth. Altogether, he cautioned that as long as the total stock of debt remains untouched and the interest rates remain valid, all the various schemes at financial re-engineering would fail. He cautioned that:

> we seem to be overly excited with each new fangled device – debt-equity swap, country fund, interest capitalization, and all the rest. We clutch at each device as if it can serve as an adequate alibi for hard decisions. We seize on each artifice avidly as a panacea; yet all we need to do is to look up the experience of others and read up what is fully documented in the literature (Okigbo 1993, vol.4, 136).

The debtor nations, he maintained:

> should recognize that the sheer size of their debt gives them tremendous strength, hence, a general or collective repudiation will totally disorganize the international financial system. Though no one would cavalierly urge repudiation of Third World debt, the creditors must realize that their own intransigence in the face of shrinking capacity to pay may force the debtor countries into some collective but unilateral action that may wreak havoc on the system as a whole (Okigbo 1993, vol. 4, 136).

To avoid the debt trap, it was in the interest of both debtors and creditors to reach a mutual accommodation that recognizes the need for equity on the one hand and the realities of the marketplace on the other.

On the issue of how to deal with Third World poverty, Okigbo rejects the idea of making a distinction between the rural and the urban poor (Okigbo 1993, vol. 4, 200–201). He points out that the real issue is not to raise the rural areas to the status of the urban areas that also house a large population of the poor; the issue is to attack poverty where it is worst. While rural development schemes may redress the imbalance between rural and urban income and wealth, they do not attack the problem of urban and rural poor directly. To the extent that it is difficult to use public funds to compensate the poor if they are provided either free for everybody without a means test or are charged in accordance to use irrespective of income; any reasonable effort to alleviate the lot of the poor must deliberately discriminate in their favour. Therefore, he maintains that the best way for policy makers to ameliorate the situation is:

> ...to deal directly with poverty: by providing training, creating job opportunities addressed specifically to the poor, providing subsidies to the poor in the items of most demand (food, health, water, education),

granting specialized credit facilities to the poor, and on conditions that take their situation into account (Okigbo 1993, vol. 4, 201).

While the South Commission's report makes a theoretical argument for a self-reliant and human-centred development model among countries of the South, one has to go back to Okigbo's essay (1993, vol. 4, 201) for the specifics on how this can be achieved, or at best attempted. He points out that while economic growth is necessary to yield the resources to relieve poverty, growth is not development nor should it be regarded as an end in itself. In dealing with the problem of poverty, growth is a necessary but not a sufficient condition for success. While recognizing the fact that the campaign for economic independence and autonomy is more pernicious, more insidious and more dangerous than that for political independence, Okigbo argues that for development to have meaning, it must concentrate first on the satisfaction of basic human needs of the population for food, clothing and shelter almost entirely from local materials. Such development should not depend on external assistance, but must be based on the internal efforts and resources of the country, material and human. Importing equipment with the latest technology defeats this purpose.

For Okigbo, self-reliant development is a process of liberation, both for the individual and the entire community: a release of creative and innovative talents. Development cannot be sustained unless it is anchored on the liberation and autonomy of the individual. It requires a high level of discipline by all cadres, but unfortunately this seems difficult for many countries. While accepting the economic and political interdependence of the global community, he warns that self-reliance does not ipso facto mean a total delinking from the rest of the world. Rather, it demands autonomy in decision-making, domestic management and international arrangements.

LIBERAL ECONOMICS AND THE SOUTH'S AGENDA
The case for Third World development transcends not only the issues of debt, poverty and indigenous productivity, but is also mired in the ideological face-off between the liberal and unfettered logic of the market and the practical necessity for state intervention. The South Commission's report rejects the notion that the free-market system and state-centred planning are mutually exclusive, but instead, prefers a mixed economy model in which the state and the market mechanisms complement each other. 'It suggests that the role of the state in the management of development will remain essential even if the market is chosen as the primary instrument for resource allocation' (The South Centre 1993, 106). While subscribing to this view, Okigbo points out that it is nonetheless necessary to define the extent and scope of state intervention, especially in those fields where economic and financial calculus alone cannot satisfy the social objectives of government.

This premise is also supported by Harald Malmgrem (1977, 231, 232), a one-time United States deputy special representative for trade negotiations, who argues:

> that liberalization is by itself not an adequate policy for developed countries, nor is it all that the developing countries should advocate... Doctrinal pursuit of the virtues of free markets cannot be meaningful without establishing boundaries for legitimate government action, since governments must act for political reasons. Indeed, there is no virtue in the free market without fixed rules of all kinds, including those establishing boundaries for government action... [Furthermore]...given the already existing influences of governments and the political likelihood that they will increasingly involve themselves in ownership, management, or intensified regulation of producing and trading activities, the real issues are two-fold – whether adequate investment will take place in a context of political uncertainty, and whether the policies of governments can be carried out in ways that can be considered economically efficient.

One of the key arguments of the South Commission is that the South must embrace a self-reliant people-centred development strategy that lends credibility to the vital role of government as a central agency in the distribution of social goods and opportunities. But it becomes problematic, and even contradictory, if such an ideal is pursued by recourse to the liberal economic doctrine. The commission's report points out that it is particularly unlikely that the free play of market forces would result in the growth with equity that a people-centred development strategy seeks to achieve because:

> excessive reliance on market forces can lead to concentration of economic power and wider disparities in income and wealth, to the under-utilization of resources, to unemployment, and to the wastage of the savings potential – with the result that the pace of development and technical progress is retarded (Malmgren 1997, 114–115).

Furthermore, Malmgren (1997, 232–233) argues that while 'the process of interdependence might bring overall economic gain, the market does not necessarily distribute the gains in an equitable way internationally any more than it does on a national basis, hence care must be taken to manage the relationships of social and private costs and benefits'. While the developing countries have focused on the desire to seek and maintain high price levels for their export-based primary products, there are many arguments against this. The point is that 'nations that do not have exportable commodities will not be helped, and may even be harmed. The primary beneficiaries of higher primary product prices will be the largest exporters of such products (i.e. Canada, Australia, South Africa, United States and Russia); and to the extent that high prices may encourage overproduction and substitution', the unsold surplus commodities will, invariably, drive prices even lower. Fundamentally, it can thus be argued that 'the complexities and uncertainties implicit in trade policy and economic policy management generally constitute a deterrent to trade expansion of developing countries, both in their trade with the industrialized nations and in their trade with one another'.

While the South Commission's emphasis on a human-centred self-reliant development model is as inspirational as it is commendable, it is useful only if its ideals are successfully reduced to the fundamentals as well as to the practical issues of development that face many countries of the South. This boils down to capital and finance. With a dearth of capital accumulation in the private sector and the lack of an efficient bureaucratic system, the public sector (in this case the government) becomes the primary agency for the provision of public goods as well as the major organ for investments and employment. To the extent that finance and capital remains at the core of the South's development efforts, the key challenge will always be how to reconcile the concept of self-reliant development with internal capacity of the South and the realities of the international economic system. While many countries of the South have attempted some kind of reluctant romance with externally-induced structural adjustment programmes, success stories have been very rare and the economic damage wrought on these countries have created more confusion than useful ideas. Reliance on external finance with such stringent International Monetary Fund conditionalities have overpowered the struggling economies of most developing countries, hence the shattering level of failure.

The ideal of self-reliant development must live up to its true bidding. The South countries should begin by renegotiating their developmental priorities in line with their natural and human resource capabilities. Such priorities should emphasize education, agriculture, vocational training, health care and small-scale or intermediate manufacturing that easily adapt to the most rudimentary form of localized technology. Over time the combination of improvement in human capital skills through education and training and its adaptation to the local technology will generate a reciprocal effect or critical mass upon which to build a more extended and sophisticated model of development. What the countries of the South need is not a rational or sentimental imitation of the development models of the advanced industrialized countries in the North, but instead a model that encourages an incremental adaptation of its internal capabilities to new learning and knowledge gleaned from external sources.

While the availability of investment finance is limited essentially to external sources, the South must temper its appetite for borrowing with prudence and calculated austerity. Simply put, external borrowing should be limited to capital sourcing for initial investments, after which consequent financial needs should be supported by proceeds generated from the investments themselves. If such investments cannot provide a basis for their continuous support, they should be seriously re-evaluated or dismantled. The real problem with 'white elephants' is not that they were ever built, but rather that it costs money to maintain them. Where the maintenance funds are not available, then both the initial investment and all consequent expenditures are wasted. Can the countries of the South afford this? And for how long?

THE SOUTH CENTRE: FORTUNE INTERRUPTED?

The South Centre was formally established as a permanent intergovernmental organization of developing countries on July 31, 1995. In pursuing its 'objective of promoting South-South cooperation and coordinated participation by developing countries in international forums', the South Centre maintains full intellectual independence. Broadly, the centre works to assist in formulating the South's position on major policy issues and to generate ideas and action-oriented proposals for consideration by the collectivity of the South governments as well as agencies for intergovernmental cooperation and transnational nongovernmental organizations. Currently, forty-six countries belong to the South Centre. A board, whose members are elected in their personal capacity for three-year terms, oversees the operation of the centre, approves its work programmes, assists in fund-raising, reviews the budget and yearly-audited accounts, and generally assists the work of the chairperson (The South Centre 1996).

The death of Nyerere ushered in a period of great difficulty for the South Centre, exacerbated by the death of Okigbo the following year. The last meeting of the board Okigbo attended was held shortly after Nyerere's death. Once more, Okigbo played a critical role in supporting efforts to stabilize the centre and to select a new chairperson. Had his health not failed suddenly, there is little doubt that he would have played a similar role to shield the centre from the serious disputes that developed among member countries immediately following the Havana summit in April 2000. Much of these disagreements resulted from misinformation and misunderstanding about the purpose of the South Centre by rival national leaders, including the president of his own country, Nigeria. As the South Centre struggled to reassert its institutional legitimacy, a meeting of its council of governments (member countries) was scheduled to convene in July 2001 to reconstruct the group's solidarity and purpose.

On August 18–22, 2001, the tenth meeting of the Intergovernmental Follow-up and Coordination Committee on Economic Cooperation among Developing Countries was held in Tehran, Iran. Among the resolutions that came out of the conference was the launching of the 'South Report', a basic reference and major policy/analytical tool on the state of South-South cooperation. Other resolutions included a call for the building of a broad-based partnership to include public and private sectors, the academia and civil society organizations; a reaffirmation of the role of the United Nations Development Program (UNDP) in supporting South-South cooperation and in advancing a more inclusive globalization agenda; and a proposal for an International Decade on South-South Cooperation to generate increased political dynamism and visibility in the international arena. While different models of institutional development are contemplated, the one that seems to stand out most is that of a secretariat directly under the control of local missions. How the centre is able to resolve the institutional crisis of leadership and the systemic crisis of values that it currently faces will provide one of the first indications of its ability to nurture and advance many of the lofty ideals bequeathed by Nyerere and Okigbo, among others.

REFERENCES

Bates, Robert H. 1981. *Markets and States in Tropical Africa: The Political Basis of Agricultural Policies.* Berkeley, CA: University of California Press.

Hadenius, Axel. 1992. *Democracy and Development.* New York: Cambridge University Press.

Malmgren, Harald B. 1977. 'Trade Policies of the Developed Countries for the Next Decade'. In Jadish N. Bagwati, ed., *The New International Economic Order: The North-South Debate,* 219–235. Cambridge, MA: The Massachusetts Institute of Technology Press.

Okigbo, P.N.C. 1993. *Essays in the Public Philosophy of Development,* vol.2: *Change and Crisis in the Management of the Nigerian Economy.* Enugu, Nigeria: Fourth Dimension Publishing Co.

———— 1993. *Essays in the Public Philosophy of Development,* vol.3: *Growth and Structure of the Nigerian Economy.* Enugu, Nigeria: Fourth Dimension Publishing Co.

————. 1993. *Essays in the Public Philosophy of Development,* vol. 4: *Lectures on the Structural Adjustment Program.* Enugu, Nigeria: Fourth Dimension Publishing Co.

South Commission. 1990. *The Challenge to the South: The Report of the South Commission.* New York: Oxford University Press.

The South Centre. 1993. *Facing the Challenge: Responses to the Report of the South Commission.* London: Zed Books.

————. 1996. *Liberalization and Globalization: Drawing Conclusions for Development.* Atar, Geneva: The South Centre.

Thucydides. 1954. *The Peloponnesian War.* Translated, with an introduction by Rex Warner). Baltimore, MD: Penguin Books.

APPENDICES

Appendix 1

PIUS NWABUFO CHARLES OKIGBO (1924–2000)[1]

LaRay Denzer

Nigerian intellectual giant Pius Nwabufo Charles Okigbo – economist, policy-maker and international consultant – died on September 11, 2000. He was distinguished by being first in many endeavours: Nigeria's first development officer, Nigeria's first indigenous economic adviser to the federal government, first Nigerian ambassador to the European Economic Community and first economic adviser to the defunct Biafran government. For his pioneering work in economic planning, he received numerous national honours and honorary doctorate degrees.

Born in 1924 in the small forest village of Ojoto near Onitsha, in what is now Anambra State in southeastern Nigeria, he belonged to the emergent Igbo elite that flourished during the colonial era. His grandfather was one of the earliest warrant chiefs – leaders the British colonial administration superimposed on the indigenous political system of Igboland. Like many of these chiefs, his grandfather saw the opportunities for advancement inherent in converting to Catholicism, which may well have also cloaked a subtle form of cultural resistance to the Anglican colonial project. James Okoloafor Okigbo, became a headmaster, who served in elementary mission schools in southeastern Nigeria. He ensured that his young son Pius received the best Catholic education available at the time in Eastern Nigeria, from elementary school to Christ the King Grammar School in Onitsha, the first full-fledged Catholic secondary school east of the Niger. Even then, the young Pius Okigbo stood apart from his generation of young independent-minded and talented nation builders.

[1] Originally published in *P. A. S. News and Events* 11(2), 2001:4.

On completion of secondary school in 1941, at the height of World War II, Okigbo joined the growing group of Nigerian youth whose ideas about their future were shaped by journalist Nnamdi Azikiwe, editor of the *West African Pilot*, whose writing maintained unrelenting pressure for 'self-government now' and Nigerian autonomy. At that time, there was no university in Nigeria, and Okigbo pursued postsecondary training at Yaba Higher College in Lagos (1941–42) and Achimota College in Ghana (1942–43), and then enrolled as an external degree candidate at the University of London (1944–48) in law and economics. At the same time, he developed interests in history, art, philosophy and literature. With his B.Sc. degree in hand, he joined the Nigerian civil service, becoming its first indigenous development officer. As a young cadet, he participated in making policy for unprecedented postwar expansion in agricultural and industrial projects, launched by a colonial government newly committed to building a modern Nigeria. Meanwhile, many promising young Igbos like Okigbo, following the example of certain radical politicians, decided that the United States offered the best chance for the type of tertiary education required by the nascent nations of Africa.

When Okigbo came to Northwestern University's economics department in 1952, Nigeria's colonial government had set a timetable for handing over political power to Nigerians, including the indigenization of the civil service. After completing his MA in 1954, Okigbo went to Oxford University for a year. In 1956 he returned to Northwestern as an exchange lecturer and to complete his dissertation, 'Capital Formation in a Developing Economy,' a pioneering study in modern African economics. He became Northwestern's first African PhD. During his studies he was mentored by Melville and Frances Herskovits, who guided his graduate career and helped him secure several grants. They talked at length about research conditions in West Africa, confrontations with the British administration and most emphatically about the progress of African nationalism and the struggle for autonomy.

Following a postdoctoral fellowship at Nuffield College in Oxford, Okigbo returned to Nigeria in 1958 and joined a select group of young professionals dedicated to the task of nation building. He helped to prepare the First National Development Plan that laid the foundation for prosperity in the First Republic. By 1965 the average national growth was 6.7 percent, compared with the original projected rate of 5.1 percent. During this period of astonishing economic growth, Okigbo also headed the negotiating team of the federal government to the European Economic Community and was suc-cessful in securing favourable trading terms for Nigeria.

When the army overthrew the First Republic in 1966, hopes for Nigeria's bright future faded as the nation collapsed first into ethnic conflict and then civil war. A patriotic Igbo, Okigbo served the rebel Biafran government as economic adviser until its demise in 1970. Although he could have carried out assignments overseas, like his brother, Christopher Okigbo, viewed by many as the most important Nigerian poet of his generation, he chose to risk his life on the homefront. To Pius's everlasting sorrow, Christopher Okigbo was killed in battle during the first month of the war.

Although this marked the end of his active career in government, Pius Okigbo continued to serve on public boards and take on national assignments for the remainder of his life. He turned to business and international consultancy, gaining international renown. Among his many attainments, he was a member of the United Nations Panel of Experts on the Institute of Economic Development for Africa in 1962, a member of the External Advisory Board at the Organization of Economic Cooperation and Development in Paris (1963–66) and a member of the South Commission (1987–90). He was a close friend of Julius Nyerere and other leaders in the Third World. His scholarly output was larger than that of many full-time academics. Among his many publications were *Nigerian National Accounts* (1952); *Nigerian Public Finance* (1965); *Africa and the Common Market* (1967); and *Nigerian Financial System, Structure and Growth* (1981). He was also coauthor of *Challenge to the South, a Report of the South Commission* (1990).

He helped to lay the groundwork for Nigerian economic policy, and the intellectual weight of his ideas has been felt by every Nigerian government through today. He insisted that economic policy should focus on the development of human capital and never wavered from the belief that government policy should enhance the living standards and happiness of ordinary men and women. To this end, he castigated the International Monetary Fund and the World Bank for promulgating development programs that diminished the dignity and happiness of people in Africa and the Third World. Even more courageously, at home he attacked corruption and mismanagement of state resources as major obstacles to national economic growth. In 1994, as head of a public panel to investigate fraud in high places, he exposed a major scandal involving the disappearance of $12.8 million in oil revenue from windfall sales during the Gulf War. To this day, that report remains unpublished and the money unaccounted for.

With the ruins of the Nigerian economy lying all around them, many Nigerians of Okigbo's generation have expressed despair that the Nigeria of today is the Nigeria of their dreams. Yet, rather than join the exodus from the nation, they have remained and continued to serve it. Through their lives of selfless dedication and incorruptible spirit, they continue to remind their fellow citizens of what the original dream of the new nation of Nigeria meant and offer hope for its resuscitation.

Appendix 2

RETHINKING OKIGBO WITHIN THE FRAMEWORK OF CONTEMPORARY AFRICAN POLICY

Rapporteur's Report

Henry Dougan

The conference on Vision and Policy in Nigerian Economics: The Legacy of Pius Okigbo, organized by the Program of African Studies on June 8–9, 2001, celebrated the life of the eminent economist and internationalist Pius Okigbo as an Igbo spokesman, a Nigerian nationalist, an African elder and Northwestern University's first African Ph.D. Participants included diplomats, scholars and other interested persons from both Nigeria and the United States. His Excellency, Chief Arthur C. I. Mbanefo, Ambassador and Permanent Representative of the Federal Republic of Nigeria to the United Nations, delivered the moving keynote address, which also served as the annual Toward Freedom/William B. Lloyd Lecture. Several poignant tributes were made: Professor Sterling Stuckey, the distinguished historian, for whom Okigbo, then a young lecturer, served as mentor during his studies at Northwestern, described the impact of Okigbo on his intellectual development; Dr. Sylvester Ugoh, former vice-presidential candidate in the 1993 federal Nigerian election and a business associate of Okigbo, emphasized Okigbo's legacy not only as an Igbo patriot but also as a Nigerian nationalist; Pius Okigbo, Jr., the eldest son of Okigbo, highlighted his father's devotion to his family and intellectual life.

The papers presented at the conference reconsidered the life and works of Pius Okigbo against the background of contemporary conditions in Nigeria and Africa. They not only reconsidered and illuminated the many dimensions of Okigbo's copious intellectual output but also set them within the broader framework of the problems that plague contemporary African states and societies.

The erosion of state capacity and the crisis of the state in Nigeria, and in Africa generally, constituted a key theme in the presentations and discussion. Several participants emphasized the state's inability to provide the basic public goods of peace, security, law, order and the right environment to allow economically efficient transactions among private actors. This was contrasted to the developmental state in the case of the Asian Tigers, states more akin to Okigbo's conception of the proper role of the state, as pointed out by Clement Adibe (DePaul University), in which the state went beyond the provision of these basic public goods to assume an activist role in the project of political and economic development.

The participants recommended that African states encourage innovation and creativity in exploring alternative forms and processes of state formation and design as a solution to the problem of the state in Nigeria and in Africa generally. Adigun Agbaje (University of Ibadan), Sylvester Ugoh (SKOUP Limited), Richard Joseph (Emory University) and Ebere Onwudiwe (Central State University) all called for various forms of restructuring of the state, including the decentralization of state authority.

The participants evaluated the need for the development of structural and institutional arrangements to act as constraining devices on political leadership, given the problems highlighted above. The review of constitutional arrangements to provide institutions of horizontal accountability and decentralization of authority were highlighted in this vein. Nevertheless, participants were mindful of the problems involved in institution building, including possible threats from further military intervention. Agbaje, Bobboyi, Kalu and Ugoh noted the forms of ethnic and regional particularisms that impede any sort of consensus formation and concerted action.

The difficulties of state and institutional reform pointed out above brought into sharp focus the increasing importance of civil society and the public intellectual in the project of economic and political reform. Participants considered possible ways in which public intellectuals and civil society could exploit opportunities created by political authority, like the creation of a panel, to take these opportunities beyond the levels planned by political authority and thus render ineffective the subversive tendencies of political leadership in policy and institutional reform.

Reno in his paper raised the problems of sycophancy and the cooptation of intellectuals by political authority in Nigeria as key challenges to the role of public intellectuals. These and other problems, such as the severe brain drain affecting many African states, the inability of many public intellectuals and members of society to rise above ethnic, regional and religious particularisms; and the lack of consensus among intellectuals were discussed at length. They stressed that Okigbo's perennial emphasis on the primacy of human capital in African development was as important now as it was in the late 1950s, when Okigbo participated in drafting the development plans for the incipient Nigerian nation and the Eastern Region government.

Given the problematic nature of solutions to the problem of economic and political reforms both at the level of civil society and that of the nation state, the more systemic solution of regional integration was discussed at the conference. Kalu N. Kalu (Emporia University) analyzed Okigbo's role in the South-South dialogue; Una Okonkwo Osili (Indiana and Purdue Universities) reviewed the limits and possibilities of West African regional integration and Souleymane Bachir Diagne (Northwestern and Cheikh Anta Diop Universities) considered regional integration as the creation of an alternative space given the crisis of the state, on which civil society can pursue its transactions, and as a mediating space between the weak nation-states in West Africa and the international political economy.

The unwillingness and/or inability of past and present political leadership to initiate and consolidate such reforms raised the issue of the chasm between the interests and preferences of the political elite and those of the populace, enunciated clearly by Jane Guyer (director of the Program of African Studies) in her contribution to the roundtable discussion. Ugoh, Hamidu Bobboyi (Arewa House), William Reno (Northwestern University), Agbaje, Joseph and Onwudiwe commented on the corrupt and autocratic nature of political authority, which in its extreme forms resulted in the privatization of the state, the use of disorder, confusion and violence as political instruments and the manipulation of otherwise useful institutions like panels of inquiry for economically inefficient political ends.

This conference successfully reclaimed Pius Okigbo. The papers and commentary showed the continuing relevance of his works, some of the most important written in the 1960s and 1970s, to the present African condition. The scope of the discussions ranged from micro issues such as the intricacies of central bank independence and non-budgetary funds to the more macro issues of regional integration and the South-South dialogue. It covered core theoretical issues in the political economy of economic and political development such as the dilemma of state capacity – how to endow the state with enough capacity to carry out its functions without its being able and/or willing to use such capacity to harm its citizens; the relative importance of structure and agency in economic and political reform; and the potential effects of integration on states and societies. It also considered the key methodological question of the problems of analysis based on statistical data, especially in the study of political and economic phenomena in Africa, given the inadequacies of the collection of statistical data on the continent. Wolfgang P. Stolper (emeritus professor, University of Michigan), whose memoir (delivered in abstentia) recalled his relationship with Okigbo at the start of his career in government service and the difficulties of 'planning without facts' (also the title of Stolper's renowned book on development). This problem continues to afflict policy-makers in Nigeria and other African countries.

The hallmark of the conference, however, might be its assembling a multiplicity of scholars, many of whom were Nigerian, to discuss the works of a Nigerian on economic policy in Nigeria and Africa generally within the broad political and economic problems facing African states.

Appendix 3

AFRICANS WITH NORTHWESTERN UNIVERSITY PH.D.S

compiled by LaRay Denzer

Abdel-Salem, El-Fatih. Sudan. 1984. Political science.
'A Framework for Research on the Iraqi Foreign Policy Behavior towards the Arab Region'.

Adjaye, Joseph E. K. Ghana. 1981. History.
'Asante and Britain in the Nineteenth Century: A Study in Asante Diplomatic Practice'.

Agbadudu, Amos. Nigeria. 1977. Business.
'Mathematical Programming'.

Agbese, Pita Ogaba. Nigeria. 1984. Political science.
'Environmental Determinants of the Propensity to Expropriate Direct Foreign Investments: An Empirical Analysis concerning Third World Behavior'.

Agodo, Oriye. 1975. Nigeria. Business.
'The Determinants of United States Private Manufacturing Investments in Africa'.

Akinola, Joshua Akinyele. Nigeria. 1977. Education.
'Faculty Participation in the Governance of Higher Education: With a Study of Applicability to Nigeria'.

Alao, Nuru-deen Oladapo. Nigeria. 1970. Geography.
'Some Problems in Axiomatic Theory of Location and Regional Economic Growth'.

Anyetei, Sowah. Ghana. 1980. Economics.
'An Econometric Analysis of Macroeconomic Policy in Ghana, 1956–1969'.

Arasanyin, Frank Ojo. Nigeria. 1986. Linguistics.
'Tense and Aspect: A Semantic Approach to Temporal Codification in Yoruba'.

Attoh, Kodjo. Ghana. 1970. Geology.
'Methamorphic Reactions in the Michigamme Formation, Iron Country, Michigan'.

Baissa, Mikal. Ethiopia. 1982. Broadcasting.
'Radio Ethiopia: Broadcasting in a Multi-ethnic Society, 1928–1974'.

Basanti, Rifast K. Sudan. 1985. Economics.
'The Monetary Approach to Structural Adjustment Problems in Less Developed Countries: A Case Study of Sudan'.

Bayo, Kalidu M. Gambia. 1977. Political science.
'Mass Orientations and Regional Integration: Environmental Variations in Gambian Orientations toward Senegambia'.

Bobboyi, Hamidu. Nigeria. 1992. History.
'The Ulema of Borno: A Study of the Relations between Scholars and State under the Sayfawa, 1470–1808'.

Breckenridge, Keith Derek. South Africa. 1995. History.
'An Age of Consent: Law, Discipline, and Violence on the South African Gold Mines, 1910-1933'.

Burns, Catherine Eileen. South Africa. 1995. History.
'Reproductive Labors: The Politics of Women's Health in South Africa, 1900 to 1960'.

Camara, Mohamed Saliou. Guinea. 1996. History.
'His Master's Voice: Mass Communication and Politics in Guinea under Sékou Touré (1957–1984)'.

Conteh-Morgan, Earl. Sierra Leone. 1984. Political science.
'American Goals and US Bilateral and UN Multilateral Funding Patterns: A Comparative Analysis of Associations'.

Daini, Ola-Olu Adeniyi. Nigeria. 1981. Computer science.
'An Approach to Numerical Data Base Management'.

Dube, Caleb. Zimbabwe. 2001. Anthropology.
'Between Starvation and Stardom: Chicago Blues Musicians as Cultural Workers'.

El-Younsi, Bechir. Tunisia. 1974. Economics.
'Financial Intermediation and Economic Growth: The Tunisian Case'.

Fadlalla, Amal Hassan. Sudan. 2000. Anthropology.
'Embodying Honor, Managing Misfortune: Strategies and Ritual Practices of Fertility and Son-infertility among the Hadendowa Women of Eastern Sudan'.

Forde, Enid Rosamund Ayodele. Sierra Leone. 1966. Geography.
'The Population of Ghana: a Study of the Spatial Relationships of its Sociocultural and Economic Characteristics'.

Fosu, Augustine Kwasi. Ghana. 1979. Economics.
'Choice of Fringe Benefits as a Form of Labor Earnings: A Theoretical and Empirical Analysis'.

Fyle, Cecil Magbaily. Sierra Leone. 1976. History.
'Solimana and its Neighbors: A History of the Solima Yalunka from the Mid-seventeenth Century to the Start of the Colonial Period'.

Hamdi, Abd El Hamid. Egypt. 1949. Political science.
'The Arab Union: Its History and Development'.

Harding, Gladys Modwyn Cicely. Sierra Leone. 1971. Education.
'Education and Democracy in West Africa with Particular Reference to Sierra Leone'.

Hashimi, Ali A. 1982. Business.
'Multinational Corporations Responses to Developing Countries Demands for Joint Ventures'.

Houantchekon, Leonard. 1995. Republic of Benin. Economics.
'Incentives in Political and Economic Institutions'.

Ibraheem, Umar Toungo. Nigeria. 1981. Political science.
'Political Participation Development in Gongola State of Nigeria'.

Ijomah, B. Imegwu Chukwumah. Nigeria. 1969. Sociology.
'Nationalism and Socio-political Integration. (The Nigerian Situation.)'.

Iwok, Edet Robinson. Nigeria. 1970. Business.
'An Application of Economic Service Potential Method of Depreciation Accounting: A Theoretical Model'.

Izah, Paul. Nigeria. 1983. Political science.
'Socio-economic Development and Political Participation in Borno State of Nigeria'.

Janmohamed, Karim Kassam. Kenya. 1978. History.
'A History of Mombasa, c.1895–1939: Some Aspects of Economic and Social Life in an East African Port during Colonial Rule'.

Jantjes, Edith M. South Africa. 1988. Education.
'Improving Student Learning through Enhancement of Initial Cognitive Prerequisites Combined with Mastery Learning'.

Jega, Attahiru M. Nigeria. 1985. Sociology.
'The State, Peasants, and Rural Transformation in Nigeria: A Case Study of the Bakolori Irrigation Project, Sokoto State'.

Jones, Abeodu Bowen. Liberia. 1962. History.
'The Struggle for Political and Cultural Unification in Liberia, 1847–1930'.

Kaba, Lansine. Guinea. 1972. History.
'Evolution of Islam in West Africa: The Wahhabi movement and its Contribution to Political Development, 1945–1958'.

Kieh, George Klay Jr. Liberia. 1986. Political Science.
'Dependency and the Foreign Policy of a Small Power: An Examination of Liberia's Foreign Policy during the Tolbert Administration, 1971–1980'.

Kifleyesus, Abebe. Ethiopia. 1992. Anthropology.
'The Dynamics of Ethnicity in a Plural Polity Transformation of Argobba Social Identity'.

Kimambo, Isaria N. Tanzania. 1967. History and administration.
'The Political History of the Pare People to 1900'.

Kodi, Muzong Wanda. Senegal. 1976. History.
'A Pre-colonial History of the Mende People, 1620–1900'.

Kofele-Kale, Ndiva. Cameroon. 1974. Political science.
'The Political Culture of Anglophone Cameroon: A Study of the Impact of Environment on Ethnic Group Values and Member Political Orientations'.

Kokuma, Francis Kwame. Ghana. 1982. Theology.
'Radical Nationalists in the Protestant Christian Churches in Ghana, 1949–1966'.

Kotei, Nii Amon. Ghana. 1969. Linguistics.
'Tone and Intonation in Ga'.

Kunonga, Nolbert. Zimbabwe. 1996. Religious and Theological Studies.
'Roots of the Zimbabwe Revolution: A Biographical Study of the Reverend Ndabaningi Sithole'.

Mojekwu, Christopher Chukwuemeka. Nigeria. 1972. LL.M., Law.
'The Nature of Law and Justice in Ibo Society'.

Mohammed, Abdullahi. Nigeria. 1978. Librarian.
'A Hausa Scholar-Trader and His Library Collection: The Case Study of Umar Falke of Kano, Nigeria'.

Mondlane, Eduardo C. Mozambique. 1960. Sociology. Assassinated 1969.
'Role Conflict, Reference Group and Race'.

Mowlana, Hamid. 1963. Journalism.
'Journalism in Iran: A History and Interpretation'.

Mtetwa, Andrew. Zimbabwe. 1984. History and government service.
'The History of Uteve under the Mwene Mutapa Rulers, 1480–1834: A Re-evaluation'.

Mugyenyi, Meddi. Kenya. 1976. Political science.
'A Trichotomy of Elite Participation in Decisionmaking: The Case of Municipal Kisumu in Kenya'.

Muhima, Edward Bakaitwako. Uganda. 1981. Theologian.
'"The Fellowship of Suffering": A Theological Interpretation of Christian Suffering under Idi Amin'.

Mvusi, Thandekile Ruth Mason. Zimbabwe. 1985. History.
'The Creation of Unemployment in Northern Rhodesia, 1899–1936'.

Mwanasali, Musifiky. Zaire. 1995. Political science.
'Politics, Crisis, and Rural Response in Zaire, 1975–1985'.

Ndoma, Ungina. Zaire/Congo. 1977. Linguistics.
'Some Aspects of Planning Language Policy in Education in the Belgian-Congo: 1906–1960.'

Ndulu, Benno Joseph. Tanzania. 1979. Economics.
'The Role of Transportation in Agricultural Production: The Case of Tanzania'.

Nkanga, Dieudonné-Christophe Mbala. Zaire. 1995. Performance studies.
'The Multiple Voices of the Performer and the Hidden Text: A Study of the Rhetoric of Social and Political Criticism in Central African Theatre and Popular Performances'.

Nwabara, Samuel N. Nigeria. 1965. History.
'Iboland: A Study in British Penetration and the Problems of Administration: 1860–1930'.

Nwabuzor, Elonejo. Nigeria. 1974. Political science.
'Ethnic Value Congruence and the Propensity for Integration: `Case Study of the Federal Republic of Cameroon'.

Nyadroh, Emmanuel M. Nigeria. 1981. Accountant.
'Corporate Diversification Information Disclosure and the Risk Return Characteristics of Firms'.

Nyambara, Pius S. Zimbabwe. 1999. History.
'A History of Land Acquisition in Gokwe, Northwestern Zimbabwe, 1945-1997'.

Obilade, Anthony. Nigeria. 1976. Linguistics.
'The Nominal Phrase in West African Pidgin English (Nigeria)'.

Ogbechie, Sylvester Okwunodu. Nigeria. 2000. Art History.
'Ben Enwonwu and the Constitution of Modernity in 20th Century Nigerian Art.

Okigbo, Pius Nwabufo Charles. Nigeria. 1956. Economics.
'Capital Formation in a Developing Economy'.

Oklu, Samuel Kwaku. Nigeria. 1976. Philosophy.
'The Premise of Choice, a Critical Inquiry into the Efficacy of Modern Socio-cultural Theory with Special Reference to the Problem of an Ideology of Socio-Cultural Reconstruction in Para-Colonial Africa'.

Okonkwo, Una Madeleine. Nigeria. 1999. Economics.
'Migrants and Housing Investments: Theory and Evidence from Nigeria'.

Ola, Israel Opeyemi. Nigeria. 1963. Political science.
'The Conditions Essential for Corporation in Regional Organizations'.

Oladebo, Samson Adebayo. Nigeria. 1979. Education.
'An Investigation of Job Satisfaction and Dissatisfaction among the Teachers in Secondary Institutions in Kano State, Nigeria'.

Olagunju, David Olarewaju. Nigeria. 1981. Engineering.
'Bifurcation and Stability of Propagating Oscillatory Flames'.

Osadebe, Oseloka O. Nigeria. 1981. Theatre.
'The Development of the Igbo Masqueraders as a Dramatic Character'.

Owusu-Ansah, David. Ghana. 1986. History.
'A Talismanic Tradition: Muslims in Early 19th Century Kumase'.

Payanzo, Ntsomo. Zaire/Congo. 1974. Sociology.
'Student Movements in The Congo (Zaire)'.

Samatar, Said. Somalia. 1979. History.
'Poetry in Somali Politics: The Case of Sayyid Mohammad Abdille Hasan'.

Sanusi, Haroun. Nigeria. 1983. Political science.
'State and Capitalist Development in Nigeria: A Political Economy'.

Sawyer, Amos. Liberia. 1973. Political science.
'Social Stratification and Orientations to National Development in Liberia'.

Shear, Keith Spencer. South Africa. 1998. History.
'Constituting a State in South Africa: The Dialectics of Policing, 1900-1939'.

Shekwo, Joseph Amali Yusuf. 1985. Mass Communications.
'Understanding Gbagyi Folktales: Premises for Targeting Salient Electronic Mass Media Programs'.

Soremekun, Fola. Nigeria. 1966. History.
'A History of the American Board Mission in Angola, 1880-1940'.

Soro, Tenema Moise. Ivory Coast. 1986. Linguistics.
'On Senari Tense and Aspect: An Analysis of the Cebarri of Korhogo'.

Stevens, Augustine. Sierra Leone. 1975. Political science.
'African-American Political Orientations and their Social Antecedents: A Case Study of Springfield, Illinois'.

Suleiman, Sabo Kurawa. Nigeria. 1984. Political Science.
'The Impact of the Policy of Relocation on the Inhabitants of the Federal Capital Territory (F.C.T.), Abuja, Nigeria: A Case Study of the Politics of Local Interests'.

Turkson, Adolphus. Ghana. 1972. Music.
'Asafo Music: A Study of Traditional Music Style of Ghana with Special Reference to the Role of Tone Language in Choral Music involving Structural and Harmonic Analysis'.

Uchendu, Victor Chikezie. Nigeria. 1966. Anthropology.
'Seasonal Agricultural Labor among the Navaho Indians: A Study in Socio-economic Transition'.

Ukaegbu, Chikwendu Christian. Nigeria. 1982. Sociology.
'An Investigation of Job Satisfaction and Dissatisfaction among the Teachers in Secondary Institutions in Kano State, Nigeria'.

Umar, Muhammad Sani. Nigeria. 1997. History and Literature of Religion.
'Muslims' Intellectual Responses to British Colonialism in Northern Nigeria, 1903–1945'.

Wali, Obiajunwa. Nigeria. 1967. English literature.
'The Negro in English Literature with Special Reference to the Eighteenth and Early Nineteenth Century'.

Woldemikael, Taklemariam. 1980. Sociology.
'Maintenance and Change of Status in a Migrant Community: Haitians in Evanston, Illinois'.

Zake, Sejjengo Joshua. Uganda. 1962. Anthropology.
'Approaches to the Study of Legal Systems in Non-literate Societies'.

ABOUT THE CONTRIBUTORS

CLEMENT ADIBE is associate professor of political science at DePaul University. He has published widely on ECOWAS, conflict resolution, peacekeeping and United States policy in Africa during the Clinton presidency.

ADIGUN AGBAJE is professor of politics at the University of Ibadan and associate fellow of the Development Policy Center, Ibadan. He is also the secretary of the Center for Policy Research Trust (Ibadan); director of the Center for Social Science Research and Development (Ikorodu, Nigeria) and a member of the board of trustees of the Goree Institute, Senegal and the Institute of Social Science and Administration, Ibadan. Currently, he is coordinating a research network on the state of civil society in West Africa for the African Center for Democratic Governance (Abuja) and a project on positive leadership in Nigeria for the Center for Social Science Research and Development. He is the author of *The Nigerian Press, Hegemony and the Social Construction of Legitimacy* (1992) and coeditor of *African Traditional Political Thought and Institutions* (1989). *Federalism and Political Restructuring in Nigeria* (1998); and *Nigeria: Politics of Transition and Governance* (1999).

PITA AGBESE is professor of political science at the University of Northern Iowa where he has been a member of staff since he received his Ph.D. from Northwestern University in 1984. He is interested in promoting cooperation between Nigerian and United States universities and has participated in USAID-funded linkages between four Iowa universities and four Nigerian universities as well as cultivating research ties with fellow Nigerian scholars at the Universities of Jos and Ekpoma. He is joint author of *Structural Adjustment and the Nigerian State* (1997) and coeditor of and contributor to *Ethnicity and Governance in the Third World* (2001).

LaRay Denzer is visiting associate professor of history at Northwestern University. Until recently, she was senior lecturer in the department of history at the University of Ibadan, where she also served a term as head of the department. In addition, she has taught West African history and women's life history in the University of California at Los Angeles and other United States institutions. She has published extensively on West African sociopolitical history and diasporic networks in the twentieth century. She is the author of *Folayegbe Akintunde-Ighodalo: A Public Life* (2002) and coeditor of *Money Struggles and City Life: Devaluation in Ibadan and Other Urban Centers in Southern Nigeria, 1986–1996* (2002).

Souleymane Bachir Diagne is professor of philosophy at Northwestern University. Before joining Northwestern University, he taught at Cheikh Anta Diop University, Dakar for almost twenty years. His work concentrates on the thought of George Boole and Muhammad Igbal. He is the author of *Boole, l'oiseau de nuit en plein jour* (1989) and *Islam et société ouverte. La fidélité et le mouvement dans la pensée de Muhammad Iqbal Maisonneuve* (2001). In addition, he has published many articles on logic and mathematics, epistemology, the Islamic tradition of philosophy, identity formation and African philosophies. Beyond his academic career, he served for six years as the cultural adviser to ex-President Abdou Diouf.

Henry Dougan is a graduate student in political science at Northwestern University. After completing his B.A. at the University of Ghana, Legon, he entered Northwestern University's graduate school, where he studies the political economy of land reform in Ghana, Botswana and Kenya.

Jane I Guyer is currently professor of anthropology at Johns Hopkins University. Formerly, she was the director of the Program of African Studies at Northwestern University from 1994 to 2001. She has published widely on West African economies, on the basis of field research in Nigeria and Cameroon. Her publications include *Family and Farm in Southern Cameroon* (1984), *An African Niche Economy* (1997) and *Marginal Gains* (2004). In addition, she has edited several collections, including *Feeding African Cities* and *Money Matters* (1995) and coedited *Currency, Credit and Culture* (1999) and *Fertility and the Male Life Cycle in the Era of Fertility Decline* (2000).

Kalu N. Kalu is assistant professor of political science and director of the Public Affairs Program at Emporia University. His research interests are comparative institutions and democratization, citizenship and administrative theory, state-society relations, civil-military relations, state and federal health policy and the political economy of developing countries. The author of many academic articles, he anticipates the publication of his book, *Rentier Politics: State Power, Autarchy, and Political Conquest in Post-War Nigeria,* in the near future.

ARTHUR C. I. MBANEFO is the former permanent representative of Nigeria to the United Nations and the Odu of Onitsha. An accountant by profession, he has spent most of his professional life as a partner in the Lagos-based firm of Akintola Williams and Company, the largest indigenous African firm of chartered accountants in the world, which he joined in 1962.

EMMANUEL NNADOZIE has been professor of economics at Truman State University since 1989. Previously, he worked with a World Bank development program in Nigeria. He has published widely in academic and non-academic journals on economic development, business and investment in Africa. He is the author of *African Culture and American Business in Africa: How to Strategically Manage Cultural Differences in African Business* (1998) and the editor of *African Economic Development,* which will be published late in 2002.

EBERE ONWUDIWE is professor of political science, director of the Center for African Studies at Central State University, Wilberforce, Ohio, and editor of the *International Journal of African Studies.* Although based in the United States for many years, he has maintained close ties with colleagues in business, politics and universities in Nigeria. In 1997, he organized the Wilberforce Conference on Nigerian Federalism. He has coedited *The Management of the National Question in Nigeria.* His recent coauthored work, *Afro-Optimism: Perspectives on Africa's Advances* (2002), seeks to debunk persistent and widespread claims that modern Africa has regressed.

UNA OKONKWO OSILE is assistant professor of economics at Indiana University and Purdue University at Indianapolis. She received a Ph.D. in economics from Northwestern University. Her research focuses on development economics, with an interest in private international monetary transfers. Her chapter on the contribution of Igbos in Chicago to housing investment in Nigeria appears in *Money Struggles and City Life: Devaluation in Ibadan and Other Urban Centers in Southern Nigeria, 1986–1996* (2002).

WILLIAM RENO is professor of political science at Northwestern University. He is the author of *Corruption and State Politics in Sierra Leone* (1995) and *Warlord Politics and African States* (1999). These works and numerous other publications explore the internal organization and international relations of 'warlords' and other armed non-state actors. His current projects involve comparative studies of state collapse and armed conflict in Africa and the former Soviet Union.

WOLFGANG F. STOLPER was one of the most distinguished economists of the twentieth century. He was best known for the Stolper-Samuelson Theory, published in 1941, which changed notions about the effect of open trade on the economies and workers of trading nations. Austrian by birth, he came to the United States for graduate study at Harvard University, where his mentor was Joseph A. Schumpeter, whose biography, *Schumpeter: The Public Life of a Private Man*, he published in 1994. He was a member of the economics faculty at the University of Michigan from 1949 until his retirement in 1982. During that time, he went to Nigeria as one of the first Western economists to advise a newly independent African government. His experience there resulted in the influential work, *Planning without Facts: Lessons in Resource Allocation from Nigeria's Development* (1966).

STERLING STUCKEY is professor of history at the University of California at Riverside. He obtained both a B.A. and Ph.D. from Northwestern University, where he also taught for many years. An authority on African American cultural and intellectual history, his books include *Slave Culture* (1987) and *Going Through the Storm: The Influence of African American Art in History* (1994).

INDEX

www.ingramcontent.com/pod-product-compliance
Lightning Source LLC
Chambersburg PA
CBHW021904020426
42334CB00013B/475